The Pastor-Evangelist
in Worship

Books by Richard Stoll Armstrong
Published by The Westminster Press

The Pastor-Evangelist in Worship
The Pastor as Evangelist
Service Evangelism

The Pastor-Evangelist in Worship

Richard Stoll Armstrong

The Westminster Press
Philadelphia

Scripture quotations from the Revised Standard Version of the Bible are copyrighted 1946, 1952, © 1971, 1973 by the Division of Christian Education of the National Council of the Churches of Christ in the U.S.A. and are used by permission.

Book design by Chris Schueler

First edition

Published by The Westminster Press®
Philadelphia, Pennsylvania

PRINTED IN THE UNITED STATES OF AMERICA

9 8 7 6 5 4 3 2 1

Library of Congress Cataloging-in-Publication Data

Armstrong, Richard Stoll, 1924–
 The pastor-evangelist in worship.

 Bibliography: p.
 Includes index.
 1. Public worship. 2. Preaching. 3. Clergy—Office.
I. Title.
BV15.A75 1986 264 85-26380
ISBN 0-664-24693-1 (pbk.)

To *Margie,* with all my love,
respect, and appreciation

Contents

Preface   9

Part One. The Pastor-Evangelist as Worship Leader

1. Preliminary Considerations   15
2. The Sunday Worship Service   22
3. The Sacraments   45
4. Weddings   54
5. Funerals   61
6. Ordination and Installation Services   74

Part Two. The Pastor-Evangelist as Preacher

7. Preparing the Preacher   85
8. Planning the Preaching   92
9. Preaching the Sermon   109
10. Presenting the Gospel   123
11. Prizing the Pulpit   149

Appendixes

A. The Integrity of Evangelism   161
B. Evaluating Your Church Bulletin   174
C. Scriptural Reflections (Childs Memorial Service)   178

D.   Scriptural Reflections (Armstrong Memorial
       Service)   184

E.   Preaching Plan   189

F.   A Tomb ("Landmarks in the Life of Christ")   192

G.   "Who He?"   198

Notes   203

Index   209

Preface

This book is a sequel to *The Pastor as Evangelist,* which examined the pastor's personal ministry of evangelism in relation to the various contextual factors that shape the style of that ministry. Having considered the work of the pastor-evangelist in terms of her or his personal relationships, I now want to look at the pastor's different professional roles from an evangelistic perspective, beginning in this volume with the pastor-evangelist as worship leader and as preacher. I am presently working on another book that will continue with other aspects of pastoral ministry.

The term "pastor-evangelist," I discovered, is not new. Charles L. Goodell, Secretary of the Commission on Evangelism and Life Service of the former Federal Council of Churches of Christ in America, wrote way back in 1922 B.I.L. (Before Inclusive Language): "The call of the hour is for the Pastor-Evangelist, a man of flaming heart, who will be all things to all men, if he may win some for the Lord."[1]

The need is still there, for the local church is still the front line of the faith and the basic unit of Christ's mission in a world that is increasingly pluralistic, secularistic, material-istic, nationalistic, and militaristic. Such a challenge demands the most capable and dedicated pastoral leadership, if the church is going to be equipped to do the work of an evangelist in this world. Robert Menzies was on target when he said in one of his lectures to a group of divinity students of Glasgow and Aberdeen universities, "It is only when our ministers become not only preachers and pastors but also evangelists that the Church will move out of its present dimness into the light of an ampler day."[2]

The work of evangelism in the local church does not rest entirely or even primarily on the shoulders of the pastor. It is a ministry in which the entire congregation can and should be involved. The focus of this book, however, is not on equipping the laity, although there are some references to lay participation in Part One. The central subject of this study is the pastor-evangelist as worship leader and as preacher. There are many good books on worship and on preaching, but I have not come across one that looks at these two aspects of ministry principally through evangelistic glasses. Much of what I have read about preaching and worship would be relevant to our discussion, and much of what you will read in this book would apply to worship and preaching in general.

My persistent dilemma has been what to include. This is not a book on the theology, the history, or even the methodology of worship. It is an attempt to think about the worship leader as an evangelist, and in the process lift up *some* of the aspects of worship that impinge upon that role. If the book serves to stimulate the reader to think of others, then it will have served its purpose.

The intention is the same with regard to preaching, about which subject almost everything that can be said has already been said. All a writer can hope to accomplish with another book on preaching is to get his or her thoughts down on paper, a worthwhile task for the writer and for whoever is interested in what he or she has to say on the subject. I had no intention of trying to reinvent the wheel with another book on preaching. The justification of this book, if there is any, is that it attempts to view preaching from one particular perspective, that of the pastor-evangelist.

It must also be understood that this is not a book on the theology of evangelism, on which subject I have expressed my thoughts in *Service Evangelism* and *The Pastor as Evangelist*. There is, of course, a theology reflected throughout most of the book, and especially in chapters 7, 10, and

11. It is impossible to write on such a subject without revealing one's own theology and style of ministry. A pastor's practice of ministry is inescapably shaped by theology and style. For those who may not be familiar with my earlier books, I have included as Appendix A the inaugural address "The Integrity of Evangelism," which I delivered on the occasion of my installation as the Ashenfelter Professor of Ministry and Evangelism at Princeton Theological Seminary. The address will provide the reader with a basis for understanding the theology and style of evangelism that I advocate and try to represent.

Much of the content of this book is what I call "sanctified common sense." It is not presented as if the intended reader does not know anything about the subject. Indeed, my hope is that many of the reader's own beliefs will be confirmed, some unarticulated thoughts clarified, and perhaps some new ideas discovered or stimulated in the process. I also hope the reader will feel that what is presented is relevant, reasonable, logical, and clear. The fact that something is true does not make it trite, nor does the fact that it is logical mean that it would have been otherwise obvious. There is a difference between "already knowing" something and already *doing* it. I have observed too many negative examples to believe that very many pastors are thinking seriously and systematically about all of the things with which this book deals.

Many of the ideas herein have been bounced off my students and the pastors who have attended my workshops and seminars. For their frank reactions and helpful suggestions, for the object lessons they provided, and for their encouragement for me to pursue this project, I am deeply grateful. Most of all, I again want to thank my wife, Margie, for her careful proofreading of the manuscript, for her perceptive comments, and for her constant enthusiasm and gracious support.

R.S.A.

Princeton, New Jersey

Part One

The Pastor-Evangelist as Worship Leader

1
Preliminary Considerations

There are many factors that have a bearing upon the pastor's role as worship leader, factors that affect people's experience of worship and that cannot be ignored if one is thinking evangelistically. In our examination of various worship services, therefore, the discussion that follows will not be limited to the mechanics of worship but to the broader context in which worship occurs. What happens before and after is relevant to what happens during the service.

To begin with a general observation, it is fair to say that not everyone who attends a worship service understands what the worship leader is doing and why she or he is doing it. Some worshipers are visitors who may be confused by and even uncomfortable with what is going on. So might be some of the members of the church. I shall never forget a remark made to me after church one day by a regular attender, who commented on his discovery that what I said in the pulpit was based upon and related to what was read at the lectern! That might have been a commentary on my preaching, but it certainly was a shock to discover that what I assumed was obvious to everyone was a new idea to this man.

If our own members are confused, how much more so might be the stranger in our midst. Those local traditions and customs with which church members are comfortable and which enhance the positive impact of their worship experience are often the very parts of the service that lock out visitors who are not familiar with those traditions. The ties that bind our hearts often become the fence that excludes theirs. The more ritualistic the service, the more difficult it is for a stranger to understand and participate. This fact has important evangelistic implications, for the impression that visitors get from their worship experience is the most influential factor in their decision to join a particular church. Consider this rubric regarding the impact of liturgical form upon the person who is totally unfamiliar with your worship service:

The more the form, the less the identification

The less the identification, the less the participation

The less the participation, the less the inspiration

The less the inspiration, the less the evangelization

I am not opting for less ritual. I am simply pointing out a reality of which I have become aware as a result of listening to many comments. The conclusion to be drawn is not to be less liturgical but to be more sensitive to and aware of the strangers in our midst. What is needed, therefore, is more interpretation, education, communication, and initiation.

Although many factors contribute to the overall impression a visitor derives from the worship service, I am convinced that the single most influential factor in most churches, Protestant and Catholic alike, is the worship leader, whose personality and style largely shape the character of the service. Some other determinants are the friendliness and enthusiasm of the congregation, the quality of the music, the form and content of the service, the architecture and decor of the building, the impact of the sermon, the content and appearance of the church bulletin, the evidence of an active and interesting program, the proximity and convenience of the church, its denominational affiliation, its reputation in the community, the availability of parking, and many intangible factors, such as the mood and need of the individual.

The notion that most people join a church as the result of the influence of a friend is misleading and erroneous. A friend may be responsible for bringing someone to church.

The decision to join or not to join, however, depends upon what happens after the person gets there. A negative reaction to the worship service will jeopardize the best-intended efforts of anyone trying to persuade a friend to join one's church.

Granted the importance of a person's response to the worship experience, the worship leader together with the worship committee, if there is such a committee (and there should be), should give much thought to the order, form, and content of worship. These are the kinds of questions with which they should be wrestling:

What is our understanding of worship? What theology informs what we do?

What feeling, impression, and image are we conveying to strangers who worship with us?

How do we relate to and reflect our own tradition and heritage?

Is there a place in our community for a church that does things the way we do? Are we filling a need, and for whom are we filling it?

Does our corporate worship reflect a balance between tradition and creativity? Between continuity and novelty? Between innovation and familiarity? Between freedom and form? Between dignity and warmth? Between order and spontaneity?

What is the place of music in our worship? What theology and tradition inform our hymns, anthems, and the other music of the service?

How do we identify our visitors? What happens before, during, and after the service?

How goes our ushering? What training do ushers need and what training have they received?

What lay participation should there be and is there in the leadership of worship?

These are but a few of the questions that should be constantly cooking on the front burner of the worship committee's stove. Consider next the following general guidelines for the pastor-evangelist as worship leader:

Be friendly. I have stated that the worship leader more than anyone else sets the tone for the worship service, within the parameters established by the polity and tradition of the church. That being the case, a warm, friendly personality is a definite asset. A cold, overly somber preacher will not attract many new members. The pulpit is one place you don't need to keep a stiff upper lip. For heaven's sake, smile once in a while. I am not suggesting you become a Cheshire cat; I am appealing for a friendly, inviting manner that conveys a genuine interest in and love for people.

Be involved. It is extremely important that the pastor-evangelist be a worshiper as well as a worship leader. Pray with intensity, speak with sincerity, and sing with vivacity. Your total involvement in the worship experience will encourage the participation of the congregation. It is distracting to the people in the pews if the worship leader is preoccupied with her or his own responsibilities or appears to be concentrating on what is happening next instead of what is happening at the moment.

Be an interpreter. "Most Lutherans," writes Frank C. Senn, "know from memory the words and music of their liturgy. If the material is familiar, people don't need service books."[3] But what about non-Lutheran visitors? Senn writes as a pastor-liturgist, not as a pastor-evangelist. Because not everyone understands what is happening, you have to explain and interpret as appropriate. Make sure the printed bulletin, if there is one, includes the words to spoken or sung responses or creeds, or at least the page references to where they can be found in the hymnal or the prayer book. Give the congregation time to find the responsive reading or whatever it is they have to read. Put the scripture passage into its context with a brief statement before reading it. Explain what the creed is that you are inviting the congregation to affirm. In a sensitive and helpful way, the worship leader can help visitors to feel included, and the members will appreciate it, too. But don't overdo it. Too much extraneous commentary can be distracting.

Since local traditions and unique worship features can exclude rather than attract strangers, the worship leader must help visitors to appreciate why these things mean so much to the church members. For example: "This is Pledge Sunday, and we have a tradition in our church of bringing forward our pledge cards as an expression of our desire to give ourselves with our money. We invite those of you who are visitors to share in this ceremony, even though you may not be planning to join this church. If you are thinking about joining, this would be a most appropriate time and way to let us know that." Or again: "The song that our soprano Jane Smith sang at the conclusion of the sacrament of Baptism was written by our former music director for use as a musical benediction to the ceremony, and it has become a very meaningful tradition for us." Or again: "You probably have noticed the rosebud in the vase on the pulpit. Some churches, ours included, have a tradition of displaying a rosebud whenever a baby is born in the congregation—pink for a girl and red for a boy. The rose today is in honor of Timothy Jones, son of John and Mary Jones, born Friday night."

The worship leader should give unity and movement to the service and should help the congregation to feel, understand, and appreciate that unity and movement. Let them see how the various parts of the service tie together—the texts of the hymns, for instance. If another person is speaking in the service, the sensitive worship leader is able to find a way to build upon or relate to in a supportive way some aspect of that person's message, and to affirm his or her presence and contribution to the service in a manner that enhances the receptivity and appreciation of the congregation. To do that requires "a sense of the occasion" on the part of the worship leader, who is able to help the congregation to be aware of and to understand not only the interrelatedness of the various parts of and participants in the service but also the relevance of the service to the occasion and to the context of that moment in their lives.

Be a trainer. Help those who are assisting you in the service. Other participants in the leadership of the worship service should foster and enhance the tone of the service rather than hamper or destroy it. They can do that without compromising their individuality. You as worship leader should communicate to the persons assisting you in the service what it is you are trying to convey. They need to be reminded to look interested, for example, and to focus their attention on whoever is speaking. How often that is overlooked, and I must say that ministers are the worst offenders. It seems to be beneath the pride of some ministers to look as if what someone else is saying is worth hearing. Maybe they think that would be a signal to the congregation that they have something to learn from another preacher. Roving eyes are very distracting. The worship leaders who are not speaking should communicate by their eyes and the tilt of their head that they are listening intently to whoever is speaking at the moment. It helps to focus the attention of the congregation, not to mention the fact that it is the courteous thing to do.

You should also help your lay assistants with their parts of the service. Let them practice with you their scripture readings, prayers, minute for mission, or whatever they are doing in the service. Help them with their eye contact, pace, volume, emphasis, interpretation, and anything else that will enable them to be more effective communicators. Some lay people who have not had much experience in leading worship tend to read too fast and too softly. Put a sign on the lectern or pulpit where they (not the congregation) can see it: LOUD AND SLOW! Tell the ushers and those who serve communion, if you have such persons, to look at people and *smile* now and then. A certain degree of solemnity is appropriate, but there is a difference between being solemn and being grim. There is no more gloomy-looking group than a typical platoon of dour Presbyterian elders armed with communion trays and about to descend upon the congregation.

Be a faith sharer. Most important, a worship leader must be a man or woman of God; as such, your faith should come through in everything you do. Sincere conviction is far more impressive than clever preaching, and commitment counts more than eloquence. The congregation may not agree with what you say, but they should have no doubt that *you* believe it.

2
The Sunday
Worship Service

A congregation is a family of faith who gathers, tradition-ally on the Lord's Day, to worship God. Because a person's decision to join a particular church is so closely tied to his or her experience of worship, the pastor-evangelist as worship leader should give careful thought to certain key aspects of the Sunday morning worship service or services.

THE ORDER OF WORSHIP

If you want to plan a worship service that is meaningful for visitors as well as for your members, there are some general principles that I believe are appropriate regardless of your particular liturgical tradition.

Unity. Always have a reason for what you do. Everything should tie together, so that the worshipers do not get the impression of a disjointed service. You have to help people to see and understand how the different parts relate to the overall theme of the service.

Movement. There should be a flow to the service, building to an appropriate climax or conclusion. What is it you want the people to take away with them as a result of their worship experience?

Smoothness. Try to avoid awkward gaps and abrupt changes in mood. Work for smooth transitions. The use of soft music is the easiest and most effective way to do this. As you are moving to or from the pulpit or lectern, or while you are distributing or retrieving the collection plates, the or-ganist, if there is one, can improvise a few chords of background music to fill the gap. It is amazing how that lends a smoothness to the order of worship. Work closely with your organist or piano player so that you are familiar and comfortable with each other's style. To be sure, there are times when total silence is appropriate, as when the congregation is invited to pray silently, or during the sharing of the communion elements. Such moments should be part of the order of worship.

Clarity. What you do should be understandable to visitors as well as to the members. In addition to what has already been said in chapter 1, I want to underscore here the importance of explaining your religious jargon. The best way to increase your congregation's Christian vocabulary is not simply to use theological or doctrinal terms but to use them and *define* them. State the word and immediately give a synonym with which they would be familiar. In that way they can begin to feel comfortable with theological terminology. Your hope is to avoid either talking over their heads or talking down to them. You assume neither that they know a given word nor that they do not know it.

One of the opportunities to explain or underscore the meaning of some aspect of the service is during the announcements. Use the time wisely, not to repeat what they can read in the bulletin, though there are times when you want and need to underscore particular events or notices, but to share other concerns of the congregation and to welcome, explain, and instruct. What I often do during the announcements is to prepare the congregation for the sermon, when there is a good reason for doing so. If, for example, I am preaching on a difficult doctrinal theme which would demand their closest attention and deepest concentration, I may say something like this: "I want you to put on your thinking caps this morning, as we shall be wrestling with one of the most difficult theological questions, namely, the problem of predestination and free will." Such an announcement will encourage their attention, because you have shown them that you *know* the topic you have chosen is difficult.

Balance. I have already stated the importance of balance in the worship service. It is the key to an inclusive worship service. There has to be both variety and continuity. Too much of either will cause those who like the other to be unhappy. If you change the order of worship every Sunday, you will lose the love of and attachment to worship that familiarity makes possible for some. The worship leader must be sensitive to the need for a healthy balance between a traditional and a contemporaneous service, so that the congregation is kept comfortable with the service but alert. That means, among other things, being sensitive about how you introduce a new idea, such as an attendance registration, when "it has never been done before." Explain why you are doing what you are doing and how the decision to do it came about.

The principles stated above are applicable regardless of the actual order of worship, which will vary, of course, from denomination to denomination and from church to church within denominations that allow such variation. In those traditions where the preaching of the Word is a central element of worship, the placement of the sermon in the order of worship is a matter of much discussion and debate among liturgists. The trend in many of these churches has been away from having the sermon at the end of the service. Instead, the sermon is placed earlier in the service, followed by the offering, dedication of gifts, pastoral prayers, closing hymn, and benediction. This is the order which Donald Macleod recommends as appropriate for Reformed worship on Sundays when the sacraments are not celebrated.[4]

My purpose here is not to debate the relative merits of various worship traditions, or to examine the biblical and theological rationales of different liturgical traditions. My interest is their evangelistic impact, a matter with which most liturgists are not the least bit concerned. Nor were Luther and Calvin. Presbyterians are reminded by their Directory for the Service of God that in worship "all things are to be done decently and in order." The Directory goes

on to declare that "public worship need not follow pre-
scribed forms."[5]

In that spirit and from an evangelistic point of view I
myself favor having the sermon come at the end of the
service, when the Holy Communion is not celebrated. Since
the theme of the service is determined by the sermon text and
its exposition, the movement of the service is enhanced, in
my view, by a climactic order, in which the worshipers are
sent out into the world with the impact of the message fresh
on their minds and hearts, reinforced by a carefully chosen
closing hymn, which punctuates, underscores, illuminates,
or reiterates the theme in song. I find that such an arrange-
ment makes it easier to achieve the unity, movement,
smoothness, and clarity which enhance the worship experience for visitors and members alike.

I am not arguing that the sermon is the most important part
of worship. We must, as James Stewart admonished his
readers in his classic book on preaching, *Heralds of God,*
resist the extreme either of disparaging or of exalting
preaching over against worship. "The attempt to segregate
preaching from worship," wrote Stewart, "is fundamentally
false."[6] The sermon is an act of worship, not an adjunct to
it.[7] For me, nevertheless, it is thematically determinative.

THE THEME OF WORSHIP

In the preceding section I referred to the theme of the
worship service. If you agree that every worship service
should have a unifying theme, then that theme ought to be
plain to the worshipers both by their own observation and by
your interpretation of it as worship leader. A few appropriate
introductory remarks can show how the Old Testament and
New Testament passages relate, or how an anthem illustrates or amplifies the theme, or why a particular hymn was
chosen, and so forth. The main criteria for selecting the
theme include the following:

The season of the Christian year (Easter, Advent, Christmas, etc.). This is, of course, a primary consideration.

National or local holidays or events (Labor Day, Memorial Day, Thanksgiving, Mother's Day, etc.; the death of a public figure, a major disaster, a political election, etc.).

Congregational needs which become apparent in the course of your pastoral ministry or administrative duties (divisive or potentially controversial issues, a tragedy within the congregation, areas of spiritual need or for growth in faith and practice, etc.).

Doctrinal, theological, and biblical breadth (the preacher must strive to preach the whole gospel and not dwell on his or her pet subjects).

Topical interests, such as death, marriage, anxiety, peace, hunger and suffering, faith, doubt, and the Christian life.

The church program (Youth Sunday, Stewardship Sunday, Lay Sunday, Christmas Music Sunday, Worldwide Communion Sunday, Reformation Sunday, etc.).

Specific requests (people often ask for sermons on topics of special interest or concern, or on certain passages of the Bible).

Planning does not hamper flexibility. One can depart from one's plan, if circumstances call for a change. The sermon I preached the Sunday following the assassination of President Kennedy was entirely different from the one I had planned. So was the one I preached following the release of the American captives in Iran. One can change at the last minute, as the Spirit leads. In any case, one should work hard to give unity to every service by selecting an appropriate call to worship, corporate prayer of confession, assurance of pardon, benediction, and fitting hymns and special music, all of which tie in with the theme. The service should move to a climax or conclusion, so that the worshiper gets the message.

THE BULLETIN

A discussion of the bulletin, or the church bulletin, or the Sunday bulletin, to mention a few of the names by which it is variously called (in my first church it was called the church calendar), is included here because it contains the printed order of worship and is a facilitating instrument for worship. That statement assumes the bulletin is easy to read and easy to follow. Many of them are not. Some are unwieldy, too "busy" and almost impossible to read. It would be better if some of them did not have to be read at all because of the bad grammar in them. If you have a Sunday church bulletin, make sure it has the name, address, and telephone number of the church, your name, and the names of the participants in that day's worship service. There should be asterisks or some other way of indicating when the congregation rises or sits, when latecomers are to be seated, and the different elements of the service. It is not at all necessary to print the Sunday church bulletin. Most churches cannot afford to do so. A mimeographed bulletin, neatly and attractively laid out, can be just as effective and much less expensive. But whether it is printed or mimeographed, give attention to its form and content, for it can be an aid to your evangelistic ministry.

My preministry background in public relations and advertising predisposes me to be lovingly critical of some of the church literature I encounter, including many Sunday church bulletins. Feeling the need to make my students aware of the importance of giving attention to this highly useful medium of communication, I have developed an instrument (Appendix B) for evaluating a church bulletin from an evangelistic perspective. There are forty items (forty-five for a communion service), each one having an assigned numerical value of from 1 to 5 points. The maximum potential score is 116 points (130 for a communion service). There is considerable leeway in the "Excellent" to "Just About Perfect" categories in order to make allowances for nonapplicable items.

The items are divided into five different categories (six with communion) to enable a church to pinpoint more easily the areas where there is room for improvement. A random sample of the bulletins from one hundred different churches of various denominations revealed the startling fact that 73 percent of all bulletins were rated *less* than "Good." The complete breakdown of scores was as follows:

Score	Percentage	Rating
107–116	1	Just About Perfect
101–108	2	Excellent
93–100	7	Very Good
85–92	17	Good
77–84	19	Fair
69–76	19	Poor
68 or below	35	Very Poor

It is important to realize that *all* bulletins could be upgraded very easily with a few simple additions. A good bulletin is not a matter of money. The one "Just About Perfect" bulletin belonged to a very small, semirural church.

A study of the bulletins according to the frequency of omitted items produced the information on the opposite page.

More than a third of the bulletins did not include the address of the church, half did not show the telephone number of the church (or of the pastor), and almost half did not have any note of welcome to visitors. Yet we would assume these items would be found in every church bulletin. For a complete breakdown by category of items omitted, see Appendix B.

It is interesting to note that many church bulletins are more deficient in the summer months than in the winter months. Undoubtedly that is because many of the usual kinds of information are excluded when the program is curtailed during vacation time. That is not the way it ought to be, however. It is during the summer months that the information becomes all the more important, as visitors may have no idea when or how to join the church, what the

Percent of Churches	Item Omitted
86	Area code (not included with phone number)
82	Information for those seeking pastoral care
82	Sermon topic, text, and scripture passages for next Sunday
81	Words of creeds and responses, or page numbers
79	Church "slogan" or statement of purpose
76	Indication of "debts" or "trespasses"
76	Information about joining the church
72	Christian education offerings (times and/or classes)
68	Request to sign guest book or visitor card
67	Zip code (not included with church address)
64	Names of ushers
63	Names of worship leaders
61	Nursery hours and facilities available
55	Names of greeters

educational program is, whether there is a choir and when it rehearses, and so on.

The importance of the church bulletin is not limited to its use on Sunday morning. If it is thoughtfully produced, the bulletin can be the very best piece of church literature for callers to leave in the homes of prospective members, who will have all the information they need about the church's calendar, program, and order of worship.

THE MUSIC OF WORSHIP

Give much thought to the music of the worship service.[8] Again, balance is the key. Be sensitive to the congregation's musical tastes (which are usually not very high) and their attitudes, likes, and dislikes. Inform, instruct, and educate the congregation with a view toward broadening their knowledge and appreciation of hymnody, hymnology, and the nature, purpose, value, and use of church music.

Thinking evangelistically with regard to the music of worship includes an awareness of the musical medium that appeals to the younger generation. The unannounced appearance of a rock group on a Sunday morning might still be enough to shake up the older troops, but even the most hardbound traditionalists can be inspired by a beautifully sung spiritual, sensitively accompanied by a guitar. The challenge is to use the modern musical idiom in a way that appeals to old and young alike. It can be done.

The Hymns

Teach the congregation to pay attention to and think about the texts of the hymns they sing. Show them why and how you select the hymns for worship. Since people like to sing hymns they know, assure them that there will always be at least one very familiar hymn, usually two and often three. But point out that unfamiliar hymns will never become familiar unless they are sung once in a while. Let the visitors know what you are doing. Introduce and explain "new" hymns: that is, hymns your congregation has not sung before. Some churches have a Hymn of the Month, which is introduced with brief comments about its origin, author, and composer, sung by the choir, and by the congregation three or four Sundays in a row. It is a good idea every so often to do a Favorite Hymn Survey. You will be surprised to note how often some of the Hymns of the Month are included among the congregation's best-loved hymns. Visitors are always impressed by the attention given to this crucial aspect of worship. The following are the criteria I use in selecting hymns for worship:

The theme of the service. The texts of the hymns should add to the unity of the service by tying in with some aspect of the general theme.

The season of the Christian year. Take advantage of opportunities to sing hymns that are especially appropriate for certain seasons (Advent, Palm Sunday, Good Friday, Pentecost, etc.).

Familiarity. I mentioned my desire to choose at least one or two familiar hymns for every service. Your congregation will not object to singing an unfamiliar hymn once in a while, if they realize that most of the time you are trying to choose hymns they know and if you acknowledge that although a particular hymn may not be familiar to most of them, you have chosen it because its message is appropriate.

Is it "singable"? If a hymn is not familiar, it should at least be singable. One of my African students commented in class that in his culture the first criterion would be, Is it "danceable"? I tend to avoid hymns that are difficult to sing because their melody line, range, rhythm, or intervals are too complicated or awkward. If you use such a hymn, you should ask the organist to stress the melody and perhaps have the choir sing one stanza first in unison. Remember, you do not make it easier for visiting strangers when you sing unfamiliar or unsingable hymns. Most people are not musicians and do not read music.

To illustrate, the three hymns called for in the order of worship in one of the Sunday church bulletins in the thick file of bulletins I have collected over the years were as follows: "Glory Be to God the Father," sung to the tune St. Peter's Westminster; "Begin, My Tongue, Some Heavenly Theme," sung to the tune of Manoah; and "'Thy Kingdom Come,' on Bended Knee the Passing Ages Pray," sung to the tune Chesterfield. Of the three, the second, by Isaac Watts, is probably the most familiar text and the easiest tune to sing, although it would probably not make many lists of Most Familiar Hymns. It is not the kind of hymn I would recommend for inclusion for the sake of those who beg us to allow them to sing their favorites once in a while, or at least some they know well.

Each of the above tunes has more than an octave range. The first and the third present the additional challenge of intervals which, for anyone who can't read music, would be rather difficult or even impossible to follow. I grant that almost any hymn tune can be sung well, once it is learned, but I can testify from firsthand observation that few of the worshipers were singing with confidence that morning, and many were not singing at all. Those three hymns might have been familiar to whoever selected them, but it was obvious that they were not familiar to the congregation. What is even more to the point, they could hardly have been familiar to any visitors who happened to be there. The selections may have been liturgically fitting, but were they evangelistically sensitive? There's nothing inspirational about a congregation standing there with their mouths shut, or feebly mumbling, when they're supposed to be singing.

Frequency. Each time a hymn is sung, put a date beside it in your desk copy of the hymnal, and keep a chart of the number of times every hymn is sung. This helps you to answer questions, and it lets the congregation know that you take the matter seriously, that you have reasons for what you do, and that you do have their best interests at heart. There are enough good hymns in any reputable hymnal not to have to repeat the same hymns too often. In my last pastorate I discovered that of the six hundred hymns, choral prayers, canticles, and responses in *The Hymnbook* (1955), 367 had never been sung by the congregation. Of the 233 that had been sung (including Christmas carols), 167 had been sung no oftener than twice in ten years. That congregation was not atypical. Many church members, I find, are appallingly unfamiliar with their hymnbook. Many, if not most, of the beautiful hymns in whatever hymnal they are using have never been sung. There is a huge teaching task to be done.

Appropriate to the order of worship. Where does the hymn come in the service? Opening hymns are usually hymns of praise, but they can still be related to the theme. The second hymn is generally more meditative and often preparatory. The worship leader must take into consideration whether the hymn precedes or follows the sermon, or the pastoral prayer, or a scripture reading. What mood should it help to convey at that particular point in the service?

The text. Take a look at the text of the hymn. Some hymns are theologically dated. Some would be more appropriate for a Sunday school assembly than for a formal worship service. Many people and some pastors do not know the difference between a hymn ("Praise Ye the Lord, the Almighty, the King of Creation") and a gospel song ("The Old Rugged Cross" or "In the Garden"). Is the message compatible with your own theological convictions? What about the language? Is it inclusive and otherwise appropriate? What is needed is a balance between elevation and accommodation. The sensitive worship leader tries to elevate the congregation's understanding of hymnology and their taste for hymnody, while honoring where they are now. Move ahead, but not too fast.

Special reasons. In addition to all of the above criteria, any one or more of which may be determinative on a given Sunday, there may be special reasons for choosing a particular hymn, such as an anniversary, a dedication, or some other event in the church. Perhaps it is the hymn of the month, or maybe you want to honor someone's request for a particular hymn. In my first church we sang at the request of a family "Eternal Father, Strong to Save" on the anniversary of their son's death in the Second World War.

Selecting hymns for worship becomes a juggling act sometimes, as you try to decide which criteria should take precedence. It is impossible, obviously, to meet all of the criteria all of the time. When it does happen that a particular hymn fits all or most of the conditions listed above, hallelujah! The task is much easier if you plan ahead rather than working from Sunday to Sunday. I have saved myself untold hours by planning my sermon schedule, scripture passages, responsive readings, and hymns a year in advance. That is the only way I could achieve the biblical, doctrinal, and topical breadth I wanted my preaching to represent and the only system that would assure the selection of the most appropriate hymns for each service.

The best way to tell how well people like the hymns is by the way they sing. If they are really "tooting out," you know they are with it, as the saying goes. If they are standing there with their mouths shut, as too many people in too many churches are doing too much of the time, you can surmise that the hymn is not going over too well. By their *toots* you shall know them!

The Special Music

By planning the worship services well in advance, you can provide the person or persons responsible for the music program with a copy of your preaching schedule. The music director can then select anthems and other special music that tie in with your sermon texts and topics. As pastor, you might request certain selections now and then which you feel would be particularly appropriate. Most organists and choir directors are delighted when a pastor has that much interest in and recognizes the importance of their work.

In choosing the special music for worship, follow the same kinds of criteria. Here as elsewhere, balance is the key. Vary the menu (including instrumentally), so that the musical offerings will appeal to the varied tastes of members of the congregation. But remember, most people are not highbrow musicians. The evangelistically minded worship leader will encourage the soloists and choir to select music that moves the heart. And since most people are not Latin scholars or foreign-language experts, when the anthem or solo is not in English include an English translation in the bulletin. Inspirational music is a tremendously effective aid to evangelism, and it does wonders for a worship service.

The Role of the Worship Leader

Many people do not think about the words of the hymns they sing. If they did, they would not complain so much about the hymns. The message of the hymn is missed much, if not most, of the time. The same is true of the anthems, even more so when the words are not printed.

For this reason, the worship leader should be an "elevator operator," one of whose purposes and functions is to raise the congregation's understanding and appreciation of church music. There are many ways of going about this, including such practices as quoting pertinent parts of hymns and anthems in sermons and prayers, referring to or commenting about them in sermons or during the announcements, using them to illustrate or emphasize a point. Sometimes it may be effective to use a stanza or two as the prayer of dedication, or as an introduction to the offering, or as the closing illustration of a sermon. In the latter case, a soloist could sing it as a closing prayer, after you have said, "Let us pray." I prefer to have the "theme" hymn follow rather than precede the sermon. People get the message of the hymn better if they see how it punctuates or underscores what you have said in your sermon.

Occasional "hymn sings" and musical festivals help to broaden the congregation's awareness. Some churches, in addition to having a Hymn of the Month, set aside one or more worship services each year for an emphasis on hymns, in an effort to increase people's knowledge of and to elevate their taste for the great hymns of the church.

The Role of the Organist

Since music is such an important part of worship, the role of the organist is vital. How the organist plays will largely determine how the congregation sings. The organist should be, first and foremost, an accompanist, not a performer. His or her primary responsibility is to play in a manner that encourages the congregation to sing, not to dominate but to facilitate congregational singing. That means adapting the volume, tempo, and sound to the message and mood of the text. It calls for a sensitive interpretation of each hymn rather than pounding out all of them the same way.

When a tune is unfamiliar, the organist should emphasize the melody rather than burying it in some cacophonous free accompaniment. Free accompaniments are exciting when they are not overdone. My rule of thumb is to have not more than one "free" stanza in a four-stanza hymn, and not more than two "free" stanzas if the hymn has more than four stanzas. It is less likely to be upsetting to people who do not like weird harmonizations, especially people who like to sing in harmony, if notice of the free accompaniment is included in the bulletin. Many organists regularly use a free accompaniment on the last stanza of the hymn, having trained the congregation to sing in unison when that is done. One very effective way to increase awareness of the beauty of congregational singing is to allow the congregation to sing a stanza or two (depending upon the number of stanzas) *a cappella* once in a while, when the tune is familiar.

The organist should also be sensitive about what I call "transition music." The organ can do as much as anything else to lend smoothness to the service, covering the awkward gaps with soft background music. Such music should not be heard so much as felt. Likewise the prelude and the postlude should enhance the worshipful mood of the service in concert with the general theme.

All these suggestions assume a good working relationship between the organist and the worship leader, whose genuine appreciation and public praise of the person on the organ bench is the best guarantee of enthusiastic cooperation. Working together, they can heighten the spiritual atmosphere for the worshipers, including those who are visitors. It goes without saying that the one indispensable element is the Holy Spirit, whose presence alone can assure the kind of worship experience that will touch human hearts and change lives.

The Choir

The choir or choirs should support the congregation in singing the hymns. A choir can do much to improve the quality of congregational singing. Choir members are themselves worshipers, not performers. If they are facing the congregation, they should be mindful of their facial expressions and avoid distracting body movements. When they are not singing, they should concentrate on whoever is speaking and not stare off into space or at the congregation. They should look as if they are listening with interest. When they sing, their face language should be consonant with the music and the message. Why do so many choir members look so glum, when they are singing to the glory of God? They will hardly inspire many visitors that way.

I have already mentioned the choir's role in introducing a hymn of the month. The choir can also assist in the musical education of the congregation by singing less-familiar hymns as anthems occasionally, or as a hymn of meditation before the sermon or during communion, or as a concluding choral prayer following the sermon, or as an introit, or as a choral response following the benediction, or whenever a stanza or two of a particular hymn would be appropriate.

If the members of the choir, along with the organist, are going to accept their evangelistic responsibility and opportunities in worship, it is the pastor-evangelist who as worship leader will have to sensitize them to do so. Most choirs and church musicians are not thinking evangelistically. The kinds of things that are being recommended do not happen automatically. Someone has to make them a matter of concern and of intentional ministry, and that someone is the pastor-evangelist.

SPECIAL SERVICES

By special services I mean those worship services which are designed to observe or celebrate in some significant way a particular occasion, cause, date, or event, whether a national holiday or a seasonal holy day, an occasion in the life of the church or an event in the life of the community. On such Sundays the special occasion becomes the chief determinant in deciding the theme of the service. Here are some considerations.

Plan ahead. The dates of special services need to be entered into the yearly worship schedule. The pastor along with the worship committee must decide the who, why, what, when, where, and how of each event, to be approved by the official board if so required by the polity of the church. When a local, national, or denominational cause or observance coincides with the seasons of the church year or with an event on the local church calendar, which occasion will be celebrated and which will be underplayed or ignored? What if Boy Scout Sunday, Race Relations Sunday, and your church's fiftieth anniversary all fall on the same day? Obviously it is not possible to observe all the worthy (and some not so worthy) causes for which various organizations have designated certain days or weeks throughout the year. Much as I love pancakes, I feel no obligation to celebrate National Pancake Lovers Week! Having determined what events will be observed on which dates, you will then need to decide what the shape of the special service will be. How will the occasion be emphasized—in your sermon? by a special offering? by an innovative order of worship? with special music? with a guest preacher? by a special notice or insert in the Sunday church bulletin? or what?

Think evangelistically. Remember that special services tend to attract more visitors than usual. They often are community events, to which many people come who may not be regular church attenders or even believers. They may be unchurched parents of members of the Girl Scout troop who are participating in the service on Girl Scout Sunday, or friends of choir members who come to your Christmas cantata. If the special service is significant enough, you may want to enlist a task force of persons to help plan and prepare for it, deciding upon and enlisting the participants, helping to implement the decisions, and publicizing the event itself, always keeping in mind the opportunity to reach people in creative and exciting ways with the good news of Jesus Christ.

Consider some innovative services. A distinction needs to be made between special and innovative services. The latter may be defined as those services which depart radically from the congregation's normal order and style of worship. Many special services will not be related to the calendar, at which point they may be more properly labeled innovative. That is to say, they are not intended to commemorate or celebrate any special occasion. Realize, of course, that it is possible to have an innovative special service. Innovative services are special, but not all special services are innovative.

To dramatize the unity-in-diversity of the body of Christ, you might want to involve many persons of different races and nationalities as participants in the Worldwide Communion service, each one speaking in the language of the land of his or her birth, with printed translations or interpreters as needed. Or you might have a religious drama in lieu of your sermon on Stewardship Sunday. There is a fine line between innovation and creativity. You can be creative without departing radically from the usual order of worship, as, for example, by preaching a first-person sermon, or a dialogue sermon, or a sermon with audiovisual aids. You can also be innovative without being creative, if you use simply someone else's idea. Creativity assumes originality. There are some precautions that should be mentioned regarding innovative services:

1. Innovation must be tempered with dignity. It is still a worship service, and what you do should not offend people's sensitivities.

2. Give people options. If they are likely to be upset by what you have planned (referring not to your message but to the order and style of worship), and if you have more than one service, let one of the services be traditional, so that people do not feel deprived of their opportunity to worship as they prefer. It is to be hoped that in time they will be oper

to new experiences of worship, but it is better to introduce your innovations gently than to cram them down people's throats. Think, too, about the effect of what you do on those who may be strangers to your worship. What impression are you making? Will they want to come back again?

3. Prepare the congregation for the experience. Talk about it in advance and explain it at the time. Invite them to enter into the experience and assure them that you are well aware that this is a radical departure from their normal way of doing things. If, however, you intend for them to be surprised as part of the innovative experience, then you would not alert them beforehand.

THE BEFORE AND AFTER

What happens before and after the worship service has important implications for evangelism. Here are some of the matters that need to be considered:

Outside the church. Sunday morning evangelism begins in the parking lot. Perhaps it would be more accurate to say it begins *with* a parking lot. Adequate parking is an essential requisite for church growth. Assuming you need and have a parking lot, consider having someone on duty to help people park and to assist them in and out of their cars. The parking attendant could, for instance, provide an umbrella in rainy weather and offer an arm to those who need it. Many persons have joined a church because of the helpfulness and pleasantness of a faithful parking attendant. The pastor-evangelist knows that the parking lot is a mission field and sees to it that there are missionaries on duty every Sunday morning. Incidentally, why should the best parking spaces be reserved for the staff? I know one pastor-evangelist of a large church who insists that on Sunday mornings the staff park elsewhere, and the choice spots (nearest the church) are conspicuously reserved for visitors. That's looking at parking through evangelistic glasses!

The congregation's role. Many churches pride themselves

on being friendly. What that usually means, however, is that the members are friendly to one another. Unfortunately they may not communicate friendliness to visitors. Church members do not always go out of their way to speak to strangers. They have to be reminded to be friendly. The pastor-evangelist should enlist those persons who have the gift of hospitality and engage them in an intentional effort to foster and facilitate a pleasant atmosphere by bringing people together during the fellowship hour, members and visitors alike. Friendliness begets friendliness, and it is to be hoped and expected that other members of the church will themselves become more gregarious and outgoing. Geniality is better when it is spontaneous than when it is structured, better real than ritualized. The cheerful greeting after the service to those sitting nearby is more convincing than the sometimes mechanical handshake and superficial cordiality of an official greeter at the door of the church. The more persons there are greeting one another, the friendlier the church will seem and will be.

The greeters. Those who serve as "official" greeters do fill an important role, and they are a significant part of the church's evangelistic ministry, when they perform their duties well. They need to be trained how to identify and greet visitors and refer them to someone who can then engage them in conversation, introduce them to members of the church, and find out as much as possible about them. When the greeter is not sure if someone is a visitor, a good rule is simply to ask, "Are you a member of the church?" That way, the greeter never need be embarrassed by asking a longtime member if he or she is a visitor. Almost every greeter is intimidated by the thought of making a mistake and having someone reply icily, "I've been a member here for thirty years!" That is not the time for the greeter to retort, "Well, if you came to church more regularly, I would have recognized you."

The ushers. Church ushers perform a function that is very important to the church's evangelistic ministry. They should be trained to be on the lookout for and to be responsive and helpful to visitors. They should know when and how to introduce visitors to other persons who can follow through appropriately on the contact. The way an usher greets people and escorts them to a pew plays an important part in determining the impression those who are visitors form of the church. Ushers are the front line in making people feel welcome and at ease.

The minister's aides. Greeters are not alone in needing to be concerned about greeting people at the door. There ought to be a course in seminary in "church doorsmanship." For pastor-evangelists who receive varied and numerous messages at the church door that may exceed their memory capability, here is a suggestion: When you are greeting people after church, you may want to have someone stand nearby to jot down things you want to remember and to whom you can refer visitors you have identified. In some churches such persons are called minister's aides. I found them to be indispensable, for by the time I had been given several messages at the door of the church, I was not sure who had told me what.

Those who serve as minister's aides need to be trained to do their work as unnoticeably and unobtrusively as possible. They are immensely helpful in making sure that no member's indicated need is forgotten and that no visitor slips through the cracks. In addition to the minister's aide, there should be someone (an elder, a deacon, or a member trained for the role) to whom visitors or persons with special needs may be referred immediately, since the pastor cannot leave the receiving line.

The fellowship hour. It seldom involves an hour, but no matter how long it lasts, the period of fellowship and refreshments after the worship service provides an invaluable opportunity for mingling. Here the pastor, church officers, hospitality people, and others should be on the lookout for visitors as they circulate among the people. It is a precious time for the pastor, who must develop the knack of looking at and listening intently to one person, while with peripheral vision spotting others to whom she or he wishes to speak. Some pastors fall into the unfortunate habit of looking at or for the next person instead of the one with whom they are shaking hands. Every pastor has to develop her or his own ways of moving away from the monopolizers and of terminating the interminable. Otherwise the few minutes will be gone before one has had a chance to circulate. The fellowship hour and the receiving line are not times for pastoral counseling; they are times for saying things you need to say to certain persons and hearing things you need to hear. The fellowship hour provides an excellent opportunity for relating to visitors and bringing them into relationship with members of the congregation. One minister I know uses a tape recorder inconspicuously to make notes to himself of things he wants to remember from his contacts with people during this time.

If you wear a clerical gown in worship, one decision you need to make is whether or not to wear your robe during the fellowship hour. On the one hand, the robe makes you easier to spot for those who may wish to speak to you, especially visitors. It is also good for children to be able to get a closeup look at you in your liturgical garb and to feel comfortable with the symbolic evidences of your ministerial role. In the minute or so that it may take you to change, some of the people you needed to see may have ducked out. People leave in a hurry, and you have very little time to visit with your flock and any visitors who may have come that day.

On the other hand, you may feel that some people are intimidated by your vestments and perhaps less willing to approach you because you are wearing your clerical garb. My suggestion is that you try it both ways, and whichever way you decide will be fine, if you have good reasons for doing what you do.

The subject of our discussion thus far has been the Sunday morning worship service. I have deliberately not attempted to analyze every item in the order of worship, but rather to look at the context and conduct of the Sunday morning worship service from an evangelistic perspective. The pastor-evangelist would, of course, show the same sensitivity whatever she or he might be doing, whether a pastoral prayer or a children's sermon. In every case the same awareness of the nature and needs of the hearers would have to be kept in mind. The contextual factors to be considered are discussed in *The Pastor as Evangelist*. In the next chapter we shall give separate attention to the pastor's role as worship leader in administering the sacraments.

3
The Sacraments

The Roman Catholic and Eastern Orthodox churches observe seven sacraments: Baptism, the Eucharist, Confirmation, Reconciliation, Holy Orders, Marriage, and the Sacrament of the Sick. This book is written from a Protestant perspective, which acknowledges only two sacraments as having been specifically instituted by Jesus, Baptism and the Lord's Supper (the Eucharist or Holy Communion). While the other rituals are considered to be sacred ordinances of the church, they do not have the same sacramental significance as means of grace for Protestants.

Within the broad expanse of Protestantism there are differing views as to the significance of the sacraments, ranging from the purely symbolic interpretation of the Baptist churches to the highly substantive view of the Anglicans. The Roman Catholic doctrine of transubstantiation, in which the eucharistic bread and wine are believed to be transformed into the body and blood of Christ when the host is elevated, is replaced in Lutheranism by the doctrine of consubstantiation, which holds that Christ is really present with, by, in, around, and under the consecrated elements.

In the Reformed tradition, Christ is believed to be spiritually present in the sacrament, which is a means of grace for the believing communicants but not in a mechanical way. The consecrated bread and wine are "set apart from a common to a sacred use."

Since the purpose of Part One is to look through evangelistic glasses at the pastor's role as worship leader, my intention in this chapter is not to present a treatise on sacramental theology but to offer some suggestions that should be applicable no matter what one's view of the sacraments may be. One's own liturgical tradition, ecclesiology, and polity will determine the interpretation, form, and frequency of the sacraments, and within Protestantism there will be wide variation in all of these respects. Even within any one denomination the celebration will vary from church to church, and within a particular church it will vary with the ministrants and celebrants. No two churches celebrate the Lord's Supper exactly the same way, even when they use the same order of service. They may be similar, but they are not identical. Every congregation seems to have its own way of doing things. Therein lies the difficulty for the visitor, to whom these variations may be confusing. It behooves the worship leader to make sure visiting worshipers know what is going on.

THE SACRAMENT OF THE LORD'S SUPPER

In view of what has been said above, it should not surprise us that strangers may be confused about what is going on in the Eucharist. They may be wondering whether they are welcome to participate, and for that reason it is important that the invitation be very clear. In your introductory remarks, explain in words they can understand what you do and why you do it.

As an Episcopalian for thirty-one years I was accustomed to the weekly celebration of Holy Communion. In the "low" church where I was confirmed, there was an early communion service, which I usually attended every week, and on the first Sunday of every month the Eucharist was celebrated in each of the services. Now that I am a Presbyterian minister I am well aware that John Calvin intended that the Lord's Supper be celebrated every Sunday, and there has been among Presbyterian churches in recent years a trend toward the more frequent observance of the sacrament. There are arguments pro and con, but it is my personal observation that the more emphasis there is on the table, the less emphasis there tends to be on the pulpit, and vice versa. The more ritualistic the tradition, the less evangelistic the preaching. There needs to be a proper balance between the Word preached and the Word ritually experienced, but each tradition will determine what the balancing point will be.

In any case, the celebration of the Eucharist should be tied in with the total service of worship and not treated as an appendix. It is not something stuck on to the "regular" service. One way to avoid this error is through the use of brief transitional statements after the sermon and before the words of introduction. It is extremely effective when your introductory remarks pick up the theme of the sermon and show how the sacrament illumines or embodies it. If your order of worship calls for a hymn between the sermon and the sacrament, choose one that flows into or provides a plug-in point to your introduction.

The logistics of the service itself need to be carefully planned so that all goes smoothly. That requires some training of the persons who are serving the elements or assisting in any way. If your church is accustomed to serving the people in the pews, work out a diagram indicating the movements and stations of the participants and stating the order in which things happen. Who does what? Who serves the choir, the organist, the minister? Where do they sit? When do they stand? How do they get from one place to the next? Who leads? Who follows whom? Talk about how they handle the elements. Remind them of the importance of their facial expressions, of how they sit and how they listen. Dispel the notion that they have to look so serious, as if one can't be pious and pleasant at the same time. Encourage them to smile at people as they serve them, and to see those they know with a look of recognition and those they don't know, with a look of welcome.

Your church family also needs instruction. In addition to the sermons they hear on the meaning of the sacrament, they need to be reminded from time to time why you do things the way you do. Some churches have a preparatory service prior to the service in which the Lord's Supper is to be celebrated.

This tradition was observed in my first congregation, for whom Communion Sunday was always very well attended, in contrast to my last church, where attendance was down on Communion Sundays. The second church was historically more pulpit- than table-centered.

What about church members who do not participate in the Lord's Supper? This is a pastoral concern. They should be called upon by the persons who are responsible for the pastoral oversight of the congregation. If your congregation is too large for you to know who may be missing from worship, some sort of attendance registration is needed. You can't minister to them if you can't identify them.

Recognizing the differences and the variations in the way churches do things, you will want to consider the following questions:

Will you serve people in the pews or at the communion table?

Will you use a single cup or individual communion glasses?

Will you use fermented wine or grape juice?

Will you use a single loaf of bread, several loaves, communion wafers, or bread bits?

If you serve the people in the pews, will you ask them to wait until everyone is served or have them partake of the elements as they are served?

What will you have on the communion table? Silver trays or plain trays? White cloths or no cloths? Something else?

If elders or deacons serve the people, where will they be seated beforehand? How will they be served?

Will there be music during the distribution of the elements? Organ only? Will the choir sing? Will there be congregational singing? Will there be extended periods of silence? Music is distracting for some people who like to meditate in silence.

What is the desired mood? We call it a celebration, but we are usually very solemn about it.

What, if anything, will you say as you are serving the elements?

How often will the Eucharist be celebrated? Will it be observed on other days, such as Maundy Thursday, the Sunday after Christmas, and other special occasions? In the Presbyterian tradition, the session is responsible for the scheduling and ordering of the sacraments.

What form will your preaching take on Sundays when you are celebrating the Lord's Supper? Some preachers announce a communion meditation instead of a sermon. "What's the difference?" a parishioner asked. "About ten minutes!" the pastor replied.

Who is permitted to participate in the sacrament? Any baptized believer? Members only? Baptized children of member parents? Who and what determines whether children are "ready" to participate? Your own church polity is the guide here.

Will there be a registration of any kind? Will you use communion cards, tokens, or what? If cards are used, when and how will they be collected?

Will there be a "ritual of friendship" or "passing of the peace"? How will this be announced, and how will it be done so that visitors feel part of it and no one is uncomfortable?

What about vestments? What will you wear? If elders or deacons are assisting, how should they be dressed? What impression are they creating? What do you want to convey?

What is your practice concerning communion for the sick and the shut-ins?

These are the kinds of questions that need to be addressed. Regardless of how you answer them, you should have a well-thought-out rationale for what you do, and your answers should be consistent with your theology, keeping in mind the evangelistic implications of your decisions.

THE SACRAMENT OF BAPTISM

Likewise your administration of the sacrament of Baptism should be consistent with your theology. Since my concern here is not to advocate a particular theology of baptism but to discuss its evangelistic implications, I shall not attempt to argue the relative merits of or make a biblical and theological case for infant versus believer's baptism, sprinkling versus total immersion, or a corporate versus an individualistic view of the sacrament. Whether one believes the sacrament to be a means of grace or merely symbolic makes all the difference in one's interpretation and practice of baptism. Regardless of their theological position, most churches would agree that there should be adequate and proper instruction of adults who are to be baptized into the church and of the parents of infants who are to be baptized. For adults, it should be the climax of a period of preparation in which the significance of their membership vows and the meaning and responsibilities of Christian discipleship are clearly understood and accepted. Thus baptism and the preparation for it are an indispensable part of the evangelization process, in which the pastor should be very much involved.

In churches that practice infant baptism, it is the parents who need to be instructed, since it is they who take the vows when their children are baptized. In the Presbyterian tradition, which emphasizes the corporate nature of the sacrament, the congregation is charged to be the sponsor of the baptized child. We in the Reformed tradition find ourselves many times having to explain to people why "we don't have godparents." Certainly we would not belittle the role of those who have been so honored by a couple who ask us to baptize their child. Rather, we should attempt to give significance to the role by including the godparents in the prebaptism instruction class and in the service itself. Some feel it is better simply to ignore the godparents. I do not. Their presence gives you a chance to explain to all present, including the godparents, the Presbyterian understanding of the corporate nature of the sacrament and the congregation's responsibilities as sponsor of all the children of the church.

The prebaptism instruction of the parents is a vitally important time and a marvelous evangelistic opportunity, for it is a time for the parents to reexamine their own faith and commitment. For me, the prebaptism conferences are a very meaningful part of my teaching ministry, in which I have an opportunity to explore with a group of parents their relationship with Christ and the church. A good way to begin is to ask them, "Why do you want to have your child baptized?" Since they are the ones who take the vows, they quickly realize that their own faith is at stake, and they are ready to talk about the meaning of the sacrament and their responsibilities as Christian parents. This is a time to explain to them the history and the theology of the covenant of which baptism is the sign and seal, and to excite them about the prevenient grace of a God whose love and forgiveness embrace little children, even knowing that they will become sinners like us.

If numerous baptisms are anticipated in your church, it is wise to designate certain dates for baptisms when you arrange your worship schedule for the year. This will allow you to plan your services without overcrowding the order of worship. On the day of the baptism, the parents should arrive early enough to go over the service with you and the other participants. In the Presbyterian service the minister is usually assisted by one or two elders, who lead the couples into the sanctuary and hold the baptismal bowl and/or the minister's book, if these are used. The parents need to be told when to enter the sanctuary, where to stand, and what to do. Whoever is to hold the baby should practice giving the baby to you so that you will be baptizing the head and not the feet, and taking the baby back again without catching your robe in the process. You can show the father, if he is the one, how to let the sleeves of your robe slip through his fingers as he cradles the baby with the heels of his hands. Tell the parents not to be embarrassed if the baby cries; the congregation will be amused, not annoyed. Experienced pastors have learned not to compete with a crying baby, who will win every time! If the child is too loud for you to be heard, shorten your prayers. The length of the service is directly proportionate to the lung power of the child. In churches in which elders assist the pastor, it is a nice gesture to invite any elders who are relatives of the family to take part in the service. Be sure to introduce them to the congregation.

Most people enjoy baptisms. Baptisms are especially meaningful in the context of a worship service, and they are a powerful demonstration to unchurched visitors of the importance and value of belonging to such a community of faith. Parents are reminded of their responsibilities regarding the spiritual development of their children, and children hear parents affirm their own faith and their intentions regarding their children. There is something very moving and beautiful about a baptism, and the way a pastor administers the sacrament can greatly enhance that feeling. Every pastor has his or her own way of doing baptisms. Most pastors like to take the child in their arms and hold the child so that the congregation can see. Make sure the parents are placed so as not to block the view of the congregation. I always use a little of the water that I brought from the River Jordan, an added touch which both the congregation and the parents always appreciate. Some churches have a traditional hymn that is sung by the choir or a soloist or the congregation at the end of the baptismal prayer.

It is important that you look as if you are enjoying it. If you feel awkward or act scared, the congregation will know it. So will the baby. Admittedly, it is hard to look happy and comfortable when a child throws up on you, or gets a death grip on your lower lip, or removes your glasses, or screams bloody murder when taken from Daddy's arms. And anyone can feel awkward when a child stiffens up like a board in your arms or lunges desperately for Mommy when you are dipping your hand in the font. Some pastors stroll down the aisle with the child; others simply hold the baby up for everyone to see the newest member of the church. The parents should turn and face the congregation as you charge the congregation regarding their sponsorship of the child. After that, the assisting elder or someone assigned the role may lead the families out of the sanctuary, so that they can put their children in the nursery, if there is one, and return to the worship service. In some churches the families remain in the sanctuary throughout the service and are invited to come forward for the sacrament.

As with the Eucharist, so too with Baptism it is important to tie in the sacrament with the theme of the service every time. In addition, you will want occasionally to preach specifically about baptism, all in an effort to help your members and visitors to understand the deep significance of this great sacrament of the church, which is a witness of and to the community of faith and to the salvation which God offers to all in Jesus Christ.

4
Weddings

The fact that the only time some people ever darken the door of a church is to attend a wedding or a funeral makes these two occasions all the more important from an evangelistic standpoint. Of the two events a wedding presents the more difficult challenge to the pastor-evangelist, because the mood of the guests is less conducive to worship. It is largely up to the officiating minister to see that a worshipful atmosphere is established and a reverent attitude prevails. If such is the case, a wedding can be the context for evangelism.

Since our focus here is on the pastor as worship leader rather than as counselor, I shall merely mention the tremendous opportunity that he or she has to lead a couple into a deeper relationship with Christ and the church during premarital counseling sessions. Many of the couples who come to us to be married have only a nominal relationship to the church or none at all, and in the course of discussing the marital vows that they will soon be taking, they find themselves having to decide whether they want theirs to be a Christian marriage.

The Rehearsal

It is not as a counselor but as a worship leader that the pastor-evangelist will relate to most of the wedding guests and to the members of the wedding party. The pastor's contact with the wedding party begins at the rehearsal, assuming there is one, to which they come often from many different places and with varied religious backgrounds. Usually the two different groups of attendants do not know one another, nor do all the members of the two families. Even the two sets of parents are often just beginning to get acquainted. Most of them don't know you and you don't know them. But you can be sure of one thing: they didn't come to the rehearsal looking for a spiritual experience.

The situation can be further complicated by an officious mother of the bride who thinks she is supposed to run the rehearsal, or by a group of jokesters who think their role as ushers is to make everybody laugh, or by an inebriated father of the groom who thought he needed to fortify himself for the rehearsal dinner, or by two bridesmaids who come waltzing into the church forty-five minutes late. Here is all the more reason for you to take charge right from the start. Simply say, "I think we'd better begin. Would you folks please be seated here. Let's begin with a word of prayer." Presto! You're in charge!

From that point on, your purpose is to set a tone and style that will transform that situation into a serious preparation for a Christian wedding, which they must realize is a worship service. To be sure, you do not want to throw a wet blanket on the enjoyment of the occasion. You can put the wedding party at ease and make the rehearsal a happy experience for all. But at the same time, and more important, you can teach them all something about Christian marriage as you lead them through the various parts of the service. A rehearsal should amount to much more than showing people where to stand and how to walk. It is an opportunity to explain to the participants what the various elements of the wedding service mean and to say something about the biblical understanding of marriage and about the origin of some of our wedding traditions. For some in the wedding party it may be the first time they have ever heard these things. Some of the seeds you plant during the rehearsal may sprout and bear fruit one day. Who knows?

One thing I do know is that over the years I have had faith-sharing conversations with many relatives and friends of the couples I have married, conversations that grew out of a relationship that began at a wedding rehearsal. Some of those persons joined a church, and more than one eventually became a minister.

The Rehearsal Dinner

It is customary for the minister and his or her spouse, if any, to be invited to the rehearsal dinner. To be there or not to be there, that is the question. My own rule is to go if I feel it is important to my relationship with the family *and* if my spouse wants to come also. Rehearsal dinners are time-consuming, but they help you to become a real person in the eyes of those present, who then may be more open and receptive to you as a worship leader the next day. That in itself is an important enough reason for accepting the invitation. But rehearsal dinners also provide further opportunity for relating to members of the wedding party and their families and for faith sharing. As I write this, I am thinking of one conversation in particular, out of which came a decision on one young man's part to go to seminary. Over the years, however, I have probably declined almost as many invitations to rehearsal dinners as I have accepted. It is a matter of one's personal priorities.

The Ceremony

Inasmuch as the minister who officiates at a marriage ceremony is functioning as a worship leader, many of the suggestions made in connection with the Sunday worship service are applicable to weddings as well. Because many of the people who attend a wedding are not members of your church or any church, it is even more important for you to help the congregation to understand what you are doing. Blend formality with informality and draw them into the service, so that they are not observers but participants. When the message is for the congregation (your introductory remarks, for example), establish good eye contact and speak directly to them, rather than reading the words as if they were addressed "To whom it may concern." When you address the bride and groom, your tone should convey a feeling of intimacy and warmth as well as a seriousness of purpose. If the bride and the groom speak their vows to each other with reverence and affection, the congregation will sense the beauty and holiness of the occasion and know that they are at worship.

Many ministers like to read the formal parts of the marriage service from a wedding booklet, which can then be presented to the couple after the service. In giving a homily or a message, I find it awkward to use a manuscript or notes if I am standing close to and facing the bride and groom and their attendants. The intimacy of the situation calls for direct eye contact and a more informal style of delivery. When on occasion I have preached from the pulpit, with the wedding party seated, I have used notes. Often the message I want to convey is contained in my charge to the bride and groom, and it is usually based on some relevant passage of scripture, such as Song of Solomon 8:6; Colossians 3:12–17; Romans 12:1–2; Romans 12:9–18, 1 Corinthians 13; 1 John 4:7–12; or a passage that the couple may have requested. Sometimes the message is an exposition of the wedding vows, the introductory words, or some other part of the marriage service.

In planning the service with the couple, you will have decided which if any scripture passages will be read and whether there will be a homily, special music, a candlelighting ceremony, or hymns to be sung by the congregation. If there is to be special music, it should be appropriate for a service of worship, not the couple's favorite love song. Save that one for the reception! If you have done your premarital counseling well, they should not have any trouble understanding this rule.

At the rehearsal you will have worked out all the logistics for the service, including the processional and the recessional and any special touches, such as giving a rose to each of the mothers. You will also have instructed the bride and groom about such things as how to take each other's hand, when to look at each other and when to look at you, when to kneel, what to do with the bride's flowers, when and by whom her veil is lifted, and so on. If there is more than one minister in the service, you will need to decide who is going to do what. Things go best if the two of you are compatible in purpose and style.

Like many ministers, I do not allow photographs to be taken during the service, except perhaps one or two by the official photographer from the back of the church, without a flash. The ushers should ask anyone they see with a camera not to take pictures during the service.

What about communion at weddings? For many reasons I am not in favor of it. The wedding guests are not your regular congregation. They are not a worshiping community. Some may not be Christians. Some may not even be believers, in which case they will feel locked out when the rest of the people are celebrating the sacrament. Weddings are ecumenical occasions. Why make some people feel uncomfortable by introducing a ritual that is intended for Christians only? There has been no preparation, no advance notice or warning to the guests, some of whom are undoubtedly not the least bit ready to come to the Lord's table. As for serving only the wedding party or just the bride and groom, I am opposed to their having their own private Eucharist while the rest of the congregation looks on. Admittedly, that reflects my Protestant emphasis on the corporate nature of the sacrament. Such a practice contradicts everything I understand the Lord's Supper to be, and I have serious doubts about its evangelistic impact on the non-Christians present. I much prefer to have a private prayer with the bridal party just before they leave their dressing room, and with the groom and the best man just before entering the sanctuary.

The role of the ushers at weddings is extremely important, even more so than at a regular Sunday morning worship service. The way they perform their duties has much to do with the impression that people form of the wedding. If they greet people courteously and escort them pleasantly and efficiently to their seats, they give a high tone to a formal wedding. They need to be told how and to whom to offer their arm, how to escort and seat people, how and when to usher the mother of the groom and the mother of the bride to and from their seats, how to handle the runner and pew ribbons, if there are such, and together with the bridesmaids where and how to stand and when and how to recess and process. So, too, the bridesmaids need to be shown how to walk down the aisle with the grace and poise of a queen. The ushers should also be instructed how to help people leave their pews after the service. When the participants do what they are supposed to do, people will come away with a feeling that there was something special about that wedding, though they may not know exactly what it was. It's like putting a beautiful painting in the right frame. The marriage service is a beautiful picture by itself. The wedding rehearsal helps to put it into the right frame.

The Reception

With regard to your attending the reception following the wedding, the considerations are the same as those for deciding whether or not to attend the rehearsal dinner. Because of the larger number of people present and the consequent opportunities for pastoral contacts, you may feel there is more reason to attend the reception, or at least to show up for a while. Often your parishioners or strangers will engage you in conversation, which provide opportunities to cultivate the soil for evangelism. That is, relationships are established or strengthened which may make the persons involved more receptive to your preaching, or to your counseling, should that be needed someday. Someone to whom you have listened at a wedding reception may seek you out in a time of personal crisis or spiritual need. It goes without saying that one's comportment at receptions and other social events can be an asset or a liability to one's evangelistic ministry. Do not forget you are a minister; those who observe you don't.

The purpose of all this is to make the wedding an occasion for witness and worship, not just a sentimental custom. The pastor-evangelist does not treat the wedding guests as spectators at a marriage ceremony but as participants in a worship service. Thus the wedding becomes an occasion for presenting the gospel of Jesus Christ, as it applies to the sacred institution of marriage, which is a gift of God. What happens at the different events before the wedding helps to condition the wedding party for a more meaningful experience of worship. What happens after the wedding can build upon that experience and prepare the way for the Spirit's work.

5

Funerals

A minister friend of mine once commented to me, "I like funerals!" I knew what he meant. He wasn't saying he likes the grief and pain associated with death. He was saying he appreciated the opportunity that a pastor has to preach good news to those who are grieving. People are never more receptive to what is said from the pulpit than they are at a funeral. Some are longing for a word of hope or comfort. Some are searching for answers to agonizing questions. Some are seeking to fill the huge void in their lives from the loss of a loved one or close friend. Some are eager to hear the reassuring message of the resurrection to eternal life. Whatever their need at the moment, they are as ready as they have ever been to hear the word of the Lord.

Know What You Believe

One must have one's own faith house in order before presuming to be the bearer of that word. I could not be a pastor to a bereaved family without knowing what I believe and why I believe it—about God, Jesus Christ, salvation, and eternal life. As a pastor I don't need to know all the answers, but I do need to believe that Christ is the answer. I don't have to know the answer to the why of death, but I do need to know that Christ died for me. I don't need to know what happens when one dies, but I do need to know that my Redeemer lives. And I need to remember what the purpose of a funeral is.

It is for living persons. Keep in mind the heterogeneous nature of a funeral gathering. Everyone who attends had his or her own relationship with the deceased person or has some special reason for being there. Aside from that, the attenders may have little in common. They may be people of strong faith or no faith, they may be Christian or Jewish, rich or poor, black or white, young or old. Some may be Republicans, some Democrats; some may be college graduates, some high school dropouts; some may be executives, some laborers; some may be enjoying good health, some struggling with serious illness. What a challenge to the pastor conducting the funeral service, and what an evangelistic opportunity! Preach the gospel!

It is about a dead person. That calls for honesty. Celebrate that person's life, don't just mourn the death. Focus on the promises of Christ but don't ignore the reality and pain of death. Deal with them in the context of the gospel. Be honest, too, in your references to or remarks about the deceased. If you didn't know the person well, don't fake it. Don't pretend to know more than you know. It is risky to eulogize someone with whom you were not acquainted. Those who did know the deceased might not recognize the person you are describing. It is better to state your relationship to the deceased at the outset and use what you can of what you learned from the family and friends. Remember also:

It is to the glory of God. You are there to glorify God, not a human being. What you say about the faith of the deceased should evoke from your hearers a response of reverence and praise for One who in everything can work for good with those who love him. What you say about the accomplishments of the deceased should arouse in your hearers a desire to be better stewards of their own lives, and it should remind them that all they are, they are by the grace of God, and all they have, they have by the grace of God. What you say about the weaknesses and struggles of the deceased should point to the redemptive love of a God whose grace is always sufficient and whose power is made perfect in our weakness.

Prefuneral Responsibilities

It is to be hoped that you will be one of the persons notified when a death occurs. It does not always work out that way, but when you are informed right away, there is much you can do to be helpful. A death in the congregation takes precedence over other pastoral responsibilities, and a caring pastor will call upon the family of the deceased as soon as possible after being notified. Your purpose is to be a source of comfort and to help the family deal with their grief and with whatever other emotional needs they may have at that time. There is also a funeral to be planned, and as the worship leader you need to discuss many details with the family.

Helping with the arrangements. When the bereaved person has no other family, it may be that you can help with some of the decisions and details relating to the funeral arrangements and costs. Whether for reasons of guilt or genuine affection, families often overspend in the selection of a casket, for instance, feeling that their extravagance will atone for their mistakes or bear visible testimony to their love. Most reputable undertakers do not deliberately play upon such sentiments, but they may passively accept the consequences. After all, they are in business to make money, so why should they object to selling a higher-priced casket or providing a flower car, pallbearers, and limousines?

The death notice. You are not responsible for the obituary, but it is not at all inappropriate to remind the family to include a mention of their loved one's relationship to the church, especially if he or she was an officer. So often an obituary will list all the civic and social involvements and never mention the religious affiliation. Nor will the family always think to suggest that, in lieu of flowers contributions may be made to the church's memorial fund or to some other worthy charity. There will always be some flowers, even when such a request is included, but what poor stewardship to spend so much money on bouquets of flowers that will be quickly discarded.

Planning the service. It is therapeutic for the family if they can participate in planning the service. The process itself has a remedial effect, as family members are freed to talk about their loved one and begin to deal with the reality of death in the light of their faith, the hope of the gospel, and the love of family and friends. It is also helpful to the pastor, for I believe that every funeral service should be tailor-made— that is, appropriately related to the situation. What were the circumstances of the person's death? Was it accidental or the result of natural causes? Did death come suddenly or after a long illness? Was the deceased an elderly person or a child? The mood of a service for the young victim of a tragic accident is not the same as that of a service for someone who has lived a good long life and has died peacefully at a ripe old age. A suicide poses different questions from those surrounding the death of a soldier killed in the line of duty.

As a pastor I want to be able to see the person through the eyes of his or her loved ones. As I begin to get a feel for the person's life, appropriate scripture passages and other readings come to mind, which I can use in the service. It is best when your planning can be based on your own knowledge of the person as well as on insights gained from the family. I also want to discuss with the family when and where the service is to be held. If the person or the family has been active in the church, I encourage them to have the service at the church. I ask whether they have any favorite scripture passages they would like me to include. Occasionally they will want a member of the family or a friend to have a part in the service, perhaps to present a personal tribute, to give a prayer, or to read a scripture passage or something their loved one had written.

If your church has a chapel or room for small funerals and weddings, you will need to decide whether to have the service there or in the sanctuary, based on your best guesstimate of the attendance. You will have a better idea after talking with the family, but my experience has taught me that funerals are generally attended by more people than were expected, whereas weddings are attended by fewer. It is important to have some idea in order to know whether or not to include hymns in the service. If only a handful of people are expected, it is safer not to plan to sing. The dismal sound of three or four voices feebly upraised to the accompaniment of an organ is depressing.

The viewing. This practice varies with the locality. Jessica Mitford in her hard-hitting exposé of the American funeral industry questioned the psychotherapeutic value of "viewing the remains," which is the industry's principal argument for justifying the practice.[9] Mitford's well-documented study has revealed the extent to which "the American way of death" has been paganized by a materialistic culture. At this point I wish to state my own preference for the donation of organs for medical research and for cremation of the body, followed by a memorial service. I have come to appreciate, nevertheless, the value of having a stated time for friends to pay their respects to the bereaved family. Some families dread the thought of it, but afterward they are always grateful for the experience, which some find uplifting and even exhilarating, as they hear their loved one affirmed over and over again and experience the caring support of friends. I shall let the psychiatrists debate the therapeutic value of viewing the corpse. Though I do have my own ideas on the subject, all I want to say here is that, if there is a viewing, the pastor should make an appearance as an expression of his or her pastoral care and concern. That additional contact helps to cement the pastor's relationship with the family, which in turn will make the service more meaningful for them.

Informing the congregation. When a church member dies, it is the pastor's responsibility to see that the congregation is notified by the usual means of communication. Some churches have a telephone-calling network for such purposes, so that as many people as possible can be informed as to the time and place of the service. If the service is likely to be well attended, it is a good idea for the church to provide its own well-trained ushers rather than relying on the undertaker, whose employees cannot be expected to have any evangelistic sensitivity. If you have an opportunity to make an announcement from the pulpit before the service, so much the better. If the service has already taken place, there still may be those who have not heard the news. In either case, you can speak as a teacher to your congregation and as an evangelist to your visitors.

The Funeral Service

I am using the term generically, not in contradistinction to a memorial service. My understanding of the distinction between the two has to do with whether or not the casket is present. Memorial services can be held long after someone has been buried. The word "funeral" connotes the entire burial process, although I also want to distinguish here between a service held in the church or mortuary and the committal service at the cemetery, each of which will be considered separately.

The funeral file. As I have stated earlier, wherever the service is held and whatever form it may take, it should be designed to fit the circumstances. To have that kind of flexibility, a pastor should keep a file of biblical passages, poems, hymn texts, prayers, illustrations, and orders of worship upon which to draw when planning a funeral.[10] After having met with the family, when I am alone in my study I thumb through the file and select passages and other materials that seem pertinent, along with any others that have come to mind, and out of these I select the ones I want to use. Next I arrange them, with accompanying introductory or transition remarks, in the order I have decided to follow on that occasion. All of the written material is then inserted into a small loose-leaf notebook, which I use in the service. The file keeps growing as new readings are added after each funeral.

When the service is at the church. Work closely with the undertaker. But remember, you are the funeral director! If the casket is present, it should be closed. You want people to focus on the gospel, not on the corpse. Flower decorations should be modest and tastefully placed. The church need not resemble a funeral parlor. The pastor should meet with the family in the church parlor or a room where they can be alone for a prayer before entering the chapel or sanctuary. It is proper for the pastor to escort the family to their seats in the front pews. For larger funerals, it is good to have a printed or mimeographed order of service for the ushers to distribute, assuming you have time to produce one.

The music should be thoughtfully selected. The prelude should not be maudlin or depressing but inspirational and uplifting. I have always had the organist play hymns that either have special meaning for the family or that tie in well with the message. If there are enough people present, I like to have the congregation sing two or three of the great hymns of the church, those which have a triumphant ring and which focus on the gift of salvation and the sure and certain hope of the resurrection. If just a few persons are present, too small a group to sing convincingly, I often quote parts of the hymns as the organist plays softly in the background. I find I can read two stanzas at my normal pace in the same time it takes the organist to play one stanza. The result is an effective substitute for congregational singing, as the background music makes the text come alive. One way or another, make good use of music in the service, for its evangelistic impact as well as its inspirational effect. The unchurched persons and nonbelievers who may be present should think about their own mortality and be inspired to invite God into their lives.

I always want to be an evangelist when I preach, but especially at funerals do I want to present the gospel in the most convincing way, not only for the family but for everyone else present. It is a more thoughtful, low-key approach, in the sense that there is no direct appeal for a "decision." My hope is rather that the people who are present will hear the gospel and take it to heart. I do not assume that everyone there is a believer, and for that reason I try to anticipate and deal with the kinds of questions I know are on their minds. It is a golden opportunity to proclaim the good news to people who really need to hear it. I also try to be sensitive to the feelings of the family and others who are grieving. To be too sentimental is inconsiderate, if not cruel. Tear-jerking eulogies are hard on the family. For that reason, I often incorporate any remarks about their loved one that might cause them an embarrassment of tears as part of the thanksgiving in my pastoral prayer. That is less of a strain on family members, whose heads are now bowed and whose eyes can be closed during the prayer.

Even more often my approach is to interweave selected scripture passages, poetry, hymns, and comments into a unified message. This format allows great flexibility in planning a memorial service that is uniquely relevant and especially meaningful to the family. It also permits the inclusion of eulogistic remarks about the deceased in the context of the gospel message. The scripture passages themselves are the message and are delivered as such; that is, they are spoken directly to the congregation with the inflection they would have in ordinary conversation. In the order of worship, this part would be listed as "Scriptural Reflections" or "Scripture Readings and Reflections." For examples of this kind of message, see Appendixes C and D.

After pronouncing the benediction, the pastor moves to the head of the casket and leads the procession out of the sanctuary, going all the way to the hearse. The family may stop in the narthex to greet people or may continue directly to their cars. Once the casket is in the hearse, the pastor should go to his or her car and be ready to move into the funeral procession as directed by the undertaker or whoever is controlling traffic. Some pastors like to ride with the undertaker or in one of the family cars, but I usually prefer to drive my own car so that I can proceed from the cemetery to wherever I have to go from there. I also value the time to be alone and collect my thoughts for the committal service. There are times, of course, when the bereaved person or persons may need their pastor to ride with them, and if you sense that is the case, it is important to do so. If you take your own car to the cemetery, it is well to have an escape plan so that you are not trapped by the cars of persons who want to visit with one another. Most undertakers are very helpful in this regard. Knowing that pastors may need to get away, they will arrange to park you where it will be possible to do so easily.

When the service is at the funeral parlor. Many of the same considerations apply to services in the funeral parlor. If the casket has been open, ask the undertaker to close it before the service begins. That should be handled discreetly, without the morbid ceremonialism that some morticians inflict upon the family. ("Would you like to say a final farewell before we seal the casket?") Then the poor family members have to come and kiss and weep over the corpse. How much more difficult it is for the worship leader then to lift their sights from an occupied coffin to the empty tomb and a risen Lord. What is equally objectionable to me is for the undertaker, after the benediction, to invite everyone present to "come and pay your last respects."

The atmosphere at a mortuary is different from that of a church. Though the content of one's message might be similar, the order of service is not the same. People do not feel like a congregation when they are sitting in a funeral parlor. They are more observers of a performance than participants in worship. Some parlors have an electric organ, usually out of sight, but it would be awkward and risky to try to sing any hymns. Nor is there an opportunity to work with the organist, as one can do in one's own church. Indeed, some of the music one hears before and after a service at the mortuary would be totally inappropriate in a church sanctuary. I shall never forget one service I conducted at a funeral parlor in Indianapolis. I had just pronounced the benediction when much to my amazement there came over the public-address system the sprightly strains of "Alley Cat"!

I can sympathize with the harried undertaker who has to cope with the eccentricities of so many different pastors, each of whom has individual expectations, demands, and ways of doing things. One of my pet peeves is that I do not like to be handed the death record when there are other people around. I do not accept fees for my pastoral services, for which I feel my salary is my compensation. When people see the undertaker hand me a white envelope, they don't know it is simply my copy of the death record. I don't want to give anyone the impression that I would accept a fee for conducting a funeral. I made that decision way back in seminary, when I was thinking through my personal theology of stewardship, and I have never regretted it, nor has anyone ever been offended by my refusal. It is part of my evangelistic witness. In fact, as much as anything else in my ministry it has cemented relationships with people. It has been necessary sometimes to explain my idiosyncrasy to the various undertakers with whom I have worked. Some thought I was off my rocker, but one was so impressed that he and his family started attending and eventually joined our church.

Undertakers perform a very important service for families at a very difficult time. Some of those families have no relationship to a church, and the undertaker will ask a clergyperson to officiate at the service. When one accepts such a request, one should not simply show up at the funeral parlor in time to conduct the service, like a hit-and-run preacher. Unchurched families need and appreciate a pastoral call at such a time, just as much as the most active members do—even more so. It is, moreover, a beautiful opportunity for the pastor-evangelist, who can offer them a new reason for hope and a new purpose for living, and who perhaps will be the channel that God uses to bring them into the fellowship of the church.

The graveside service. Not infrequently you will be asked to conduct a graveside service for someone whose funeral was held in another community. On other occasions the family may for whatever reason prefer a graveside service either in lieu of a funeral service or before a memorial service. Graveside services are almost always attended only by the family and a few relatives and friends, and consequently they are briefer, more intimate, and more informal. The pastor stands at the head of the grave to conduct the service, which includes the committal. It has been rightly said that the best way to show respect for the dead is to have concern for the living. For that reason, it is not necessary to make people stand bareheaded in freezing weather. Invite them to keep their hats on, and for their comfort's sake, make it short! Once again, you want to lift their thoughts from the gloom of the grave to the glory of God, whence comes the peace that passes human understanding.

Most of the time, however, all that takes place at the graveside is the committal service, which normally consists of a few words of scripture, the words of committal, a closing prayer, and the benediction, lasting all together about three or four minutes. Even so, it need not and should not be perfunctory. Say the words with feeling, and directly to the people attending, in the hope that they will actually hear the words of scripture and take to heart your prayer. After the benediction, I usually speak to the family once more and then take my leave. It is best if they do not linger too long, for invariably, leaning on their shovels nearby are the gravediggers, waiting to get to work—a grim reminder that the world goes on.

Some cemeteries have chapels where services can be held, especially if there is to be a cremation. In the latter case, you would simply change the wording of the committal appropriately, according to whether the ashes are going to be buried there or disposed of in some other manner.

After the Funeral

As soon as possible after the funeral I prepare printed copies of the service, which I deliver personally to the family. The length of the printed version varies according to how complete my notes were, but the least that someone receives is a fairly full outline of what I have said. Sometimes it is a verbatim copy of the service. I keep a file of these printed copies of the funeral services I have conducted, along with the death records. Before refiling the scripture passages and other readings, I date each one, so that I know what I have used at each funeral. This information is useful when planning services for relatives or friends of persons you have already buried, enabling you to make every service unique and yet making it possible to refer to things said or read at a previous service.

Your pastoral services to the bereaved family do not end with the funeral. It is important to keep in touch, as the most difficult time for many bereaved persons comes weeks and even months after the death, when the shock has subsided and reality has set in, and when the sharp pain of grief becomes the dull ache of loneliness. A friend whose husband I had buried wrote me several months later:

> The one thing I can tell you is that you can cite all the passages of scripture you want when a person dies, but it's two, three, or four months later that you need pastoral help, even more than you did in the beginning, because there are days when you reach unbelievable depths of despair. . . . I guess what the whole thing boils down to is that the beginning of real grief and struggle is when the funeral is over and everyone has gone about their routine business. Let the minister return in two or three months and invite a sharing of the innermost thoughts—thoughts that you don't feel comfortable sharing with your kids or friends.

One other responsibility of the pastor-evangelist should be mentioned in connection with the larger subject of death and dying, and that is to instruct the congregation on the nature and meaning of a Christian funeral. This requires pastoral sensitivity and tact, because some family for whom you recently conducted a service may feel you were prompted to say what you had to say as a result of your experience with them. Timing and tact are essential. By all means, put what you have to say into a positive context, not following a negative experience. Be careful in your criticisms of pagan practices, because many of your parishioners have indulged in them. Many churches have prepared printed guidelines for their members, with instructions on what to do when there is a death in the family. Families should be continually reminded to let the church office know immediately when there is a death, and they should be encouraged to have the service at the church. The instructions can also include suggestions about making a will, about funeral arrangements, about gifts to the memorial fund in lieu of flowers, about the service itself, and other helpful information.

6

Ordination
and Installation
Services

This chapter specifically discusses the ordination of clergy, although many of the considerations would be relevant also to denominations that practice the ordination of laypersons to the office of deacon or elder. In the latter case, ordination and installation usually occur during the Sunday morning worship service, affording many of the same evangelistic opportunities as the ordination of clergy. There is, however, something special about the ordination of men and women to the ministry of the Word and Sacraments, and we shall now attempt to define what that "something special" is.

ORDINATION SERVICES

The pastor-evangelist will often be invited to take part in the ordination service of a friend or someone in whose pilgrimage of faith he or she has played an important part. It is always an honor to be asked and a privilege to participate. Whether the service is held in your church or in someone else's church, you can approach your particular part with evangelistic sensitivity.

Sometimes the ordination is included, in churches which permit it, as part of the regular Sunday morning service. This has the advantage of assuring the best possible attendance and gives more people the opportunity to share the experience. Usually, however, the ordination service is scheduled for a time other than Sunday morning, in which case the general principles discussed in the the first two chapters are equally applicable. There is no need to repeat them here;

rather, we shall focus on some considerations pertaining especially or uniquely to the service of ordination.

The ordination process varies so much from denomination to denomination that it is even more difficult to generalize about it than about some of the other services of the church. It is in one sense the most important sacrament of the Roman Catholic Church, insofar as it is the ritual in which the right to administer the sacraments is conferred upon the ordinand, whose ministry is believed to be in direct succession from that of the apostle Peter. The instrumental power to transform the bread and the wine into the body and blood of Christ can be an awesome burden for a newly ordained and conscientious priest, who, like Martin Luther, approaches his first elevation of the host with reverent fear and trembling.

So, too, in the Orthodox churches and every Protestant denomination with an ordained clergy, the service of ordination is an impressively solemn occasion for the assembled witnesses as well as for the ordinand. The ordination vows spoken with the sincerity of one who has been called by God into the holy ministry of the Word and Sacraments are powerfully moving to the worshipers. Whether by a bishop or by presbyters the laying on of hands is a moment of great reverence and inspiration.

Because of the inspirational nature of an ordination service and despite the diversity of its theological and liturgical expressions, it is possible to make a few observations regarding the evangelistic opportunity that such a service provides. There will almost always be in the congregation persons who are not members of the congregation or perhaps who are not even Christians. These could be friends and relatives of the ordinand, unchurched people from the community, people who have visited the church on other occasions but have never joined, and clergy representatives of other Christian churches and/or non-Christian faiths. Those participating in the leadership of the service, therefore, should be careful to convey by their words and their comportment both its sacred mystery and its traditional meaning, both its corporate character and its personal application, both its spiritual nature and its practical relevance. They can help people to understand and to appreciate the significance of ordination for the ordaining body and for the person being set apart for the ministry to which he or she has been called and for which he or she has been approved by the church.

Some specific considerations follow for the pastor-evangelist participating in an ordination service.

The work of the Holy Spirit. An ordination service is a visible and cogent witness to the reality and the work of the Holy Spirit, who continues to call men and women into the service of Christ and his church. It is a sign of the fact that God is not "dead," nor has God given up on the church. As long as Jesus Christ is Lord of the church, there is not only hope for the church but there is Christ's own promise that nothing, not even the gates of hell itself, can prevail against the church. Members and nonmembers alike are impressed and inspired by the dedication and the commitment expressed and symbolized in the service of ordination.

The image of the ministry. What an opportunity an ordination service provides to shape the image that people have of the Christian ministry! The biblical passages, the theological statements in the ritual itself, and above all the charge, if there is one, to the newly ordained minister all have a part in forming (or reforming!) the worshipers' understanding of what it means to be a minister. They hear the vows and know what a minister believes. They hear the introductory statement and have a better understanding of the biblical basis for and meaning of ministry. They listen to the charge and get a picture of the demands, responsibilities, and hazards of being a minister. The cumulative effect is a greater appreciation of the integrity of the ministry and, let us hope, a new openness to what the Spirit may be saying to someone wrestling with a decision to join the church or to answer the call to ministry. I know individuals for whom the first stirrings to become a minister came while or shortly after attending an ordination service.

The nature of the church. An ordination service is also an inspirational expression of the nature of the church at worship and at work. It is a ritual of the church, and as such it is a witness to the church's involvement in, ownership of, and commitment to the preparation, support, and certification of its ministers. It is not a matter of an individual's claiming the right to be a minister; it is the church that confirms the call, validates the training, and authorizes the ministry. Yet the church gets its marching orders from its Lord, to whom it bears witness and seeks to be faithful. Some hesitant church hoppers and shoppers might well be inspired to join the church after observing it perform its function as an ordaining body.

The beliefs of the church. As much as in any other service of worship, in the ordination service the beliefs of the church are clearly proclaimed for all to hear. The ordination vows present a succinct summary of the faith to which all its ministers must subscribe. That expression, along with the ordination prayer and any introductory or explanatory remarks included in the order of worship, provides a healthy review for church members and a helpful introduction for those who may be unfamiliar with and interested in learning about the beliefs of the church. It behooves those who ask the questions and those who respond to them to say the words with conviction and feeling, and not in a perfunctory manner. When we're saying what we believe, we have to sound as if we really believe what we're saying. When we do, God can and does use our words to touch people's hearts.

The inspiration of the service. In the Presbyterian tradition the sermon, the prayers, the hymns, the anthems, the sacred vows, the laying of hands on the kneeling ordinand, the prayer of ordination, the giving of the right hand of fellowship, and the charge to the newly ordained minister all combine to make every ordination an inspiring occasion for all who attend. The ritual has its own evangelistic impact, which can be heightened by what is said and by the way things are done. In a Presbyterian ordination, for example, when the presiding minister (usually the moderator of the presbytery) goes down to the pew to escort the ordinand to the chancel in order for the latter to give the benediction, a beautiful added touch is for the moderator to assist the ordinand in putting on her or his robe. The action symbolizes the new status of the ordinand, who until that point has not put on the robe. Presbyterian polity allows the newly ordained minister to make a brief statement before pronouncing the benediction, which statement is another evangelistic opportunity, because a simple expression of appreciation and personal faith may be the message God uses to stir someone's heart.

The importance of music. The point has been made that one of the most important contributing factors to the inspirational impact of any worship service is its music. This is particularly true of an ordination service, when a stirring anthem by the choir can epitomize in song the spirit of the moment and etch it indelibly upon the hearts of the worshipers. If the service is scheduled for a time other than Sunday morning, make sure there is a full contingent of choir members on hand to render an anthem befitting the occasion and to support the congregational singing. The hymns should be carefully selected to augment the mood and amplify the theme of the service.

The style of the bulletin. Because some friends, members of the family, and others will want to save the printed order of worship as a memento of the occasion, careful attention should be given to its form and content. This is one occasion when, for the sake of the ordinand and her or his family, the church should "do it up brown." For educative as well as evangelistic purposes, the bulletin should include the ordination vows and other spoken parts of the ceremony. The names of the participants should be included as they appear in the service, and they should be listed alphabetically, with their titles and positions, on a separate page. Many bulletins include a brief biographical sketch of the ordinand, and most incorporate a nicely worded invitation to the reception that ordinarily follows the service.

The joy of the occasion. An ordination is as much a celebration as it is a solemnization of one's call to and acceptance into the ministry of the Word. The church members share a feeling of joy and pride as they watch a son or a daughter of the church being set apart as a minister of the gospel. Their joy is contagious and an appealing witness to the visitors present, some of whom may be inspired by their enthusiasm to a new level of appreciation for the church and its worship. The obvious affection and respect of the participants for each other, the warm feeling that permeates the reception following the service, and the general goodwill that prevails throughout the occasion all help create a joyous atmosphere into which church members would do well to invite their unchurched friends and neighbors.

INSTALLATION SERVICES

Just about everything said in connection with the ordination service applies equally to an installation service. However, there are some additional factors to consider in thinking about the installation service evangelistically. One obvious difference is that whereas ordination is usually a one-time event, installation seldom is. Most pastors serve more than one church during their lifetime, and each move involves another installation service. For that reason, it might have been more appropriate to relate the principles enumerated in the previous section to the service of installation rather than ordination. The order of the discussion, however, is based on their chronology rather than their frequency. Ordination must precede installation.

In my own denomination, one's ordination is sometimes combined with one's installation, although candidates often request that they be ordained in their home church before their installation in the church to which they have been called. Whether or not ordination is included, an installation service has some distinct characteristics.

The congregation's involvement. In the polity of some denominations an installation service includes two liturgical features that are not part of the service of ordination: the congregational vows and the charge to the congregation. Each of these parts of the service can be immensely impressive to any visitors in attendance, who hear the members of the church pledge their support of their new minister. In addition, the visitors are given a picture of what the responsibilities of the congregation are to the minister and what their mutual relationship should be. Giving the charge to the congregation affords the pastor-evangelist a great opportunity to excite not only the members but also any unchurched visitors in the congregation about the beautiful and unique relationship that should exist between congregations and their ministers.

The congregation's excitement. To the joy that also marks an ordination service is added in an installation service an excitement on the part of a congregation whose new pastor has arrived. It is like the excitement of a wedding, to which those churches that go through a search process may have looked forward for a long time. The honeymoon is about to begin. Now they can be about turning their dreams into reality. The anticipation shows in their faces. Such enthusiasm is contagious, and many an unchurched person has made the decision to join a church, having been caught up in the spirit of the congregation. They want to be part of this new beginning.

A community event. An installation is more of a public event than an ordination is. It is a news item. When a new pastor is installed, it draws the attention of the community. The pastor is a public figure. For that reason, an installation attracts more visitors than an ordination service, and the evangelistic opportunity is that much greater. It is a time to win friends, open doors, share your faith, and reflect an ecumenical spirit. If you are delivering the sermon or a charge, represent the church's commitment to serve the community and be a part of it.

An ecumenical occasion. Because it is a community event, an installation service is also an ecumenical occasion. Representatives of other churches are often asked to participate. One of the participants when I was once being installed as pastor of a church was a good friend who happens to be a Roman Catholic priest. More than once I have taken part in the installation service of a rabbi; it was a witness to our common role as shepherds of a flock and an expression of our mutal appreciation and respect. Because it is an ecumenical occasion, the pastor-evangelist must be all the more sensitive in bearing witness to Jesus Christ. One does that by sharing one's faith sincerely rather than by imposing one's beliefs dogmatically.

In this and the previous chapters we have been looking at the evangelistic implications of various kinds of worship services. My purpose has not been to present a holistic study of the theology and practice of worship, or to analyze the mechanics of every aspect of the order of worship, but rather to stimulate your thinking about the evangelistic possibilities and challenges that confront the pastor-evangelist in the important role of worship leader. We must always remember that those who comprise what we sometimes think of as our captive audience are not always bound by the chains of our theology, nor do they necessarily recognize, understand, share, or agree with our personal faith assumptions.

One part of corporate worship about which we have said very little is preaching, to which topic we shall give special attention in Part Two.

Part Two

The Pastor-Evangelist as Preacher

7

Preparing
the Preacher

To begin with another disclaimer, this is not a general treatise on the art or task of preaching, although much of what is said here applies to preaching in general. There are countless good books on preaching, and their contents would not be irrelevant to our discussion of the pastor-evangelist as preacher. The topic of Part Two is not evangelistic preaching, which title would suggest a different treatment and emphasis from what is intended here. Rather, my purpose again is to examine the role of the pastor-evangelist as preacher and to suggest some of the practical implications of looking at that role through evangelistic glasses.

The term "evangelistic preaching," nevertheless, has relevance for this discussion and should therefore be defined. Is it not redundant to speak of evangelistic preaching? If evangelism is the proclamation of the gospel, how can authentic preaching be anything but evangelistic? If what one says in the pulpit is not related to the gospel, can it rightfully be called preaching? So why speak of evangelistic preaching, as if there were any other kind? "Evangelistic preaching is intended to bring people to new faith and new purposes," writes George E. Sweazey.[11] But then, isn't all preaching?

The main reason for speaking of evangelistic preaching is that those who use the expression have in mind a particular style, which has been variously described by those who write on the subject. Most would agree that evangelistic preaching is clearly Christ-centered, with a strong emphasis on the need for a personal decision of faith, involving the repen-

tance of one's sins, acceptance of Jesus Christ as one's
Savior and Lord, and a commitment to a new life in Christ.
It is marked by the urgency of its appeal and by the
directness of its personal application. The implication of
those who have this kind of sermon in mind when they speak
of evangelistic preaching is that it is something a preacher
might do now and then, but not every Sunday.

For other people, evangelistic preaching means making a
case for evangelism. A sermon on Evangelism Sunday is
supposed to convince people that evangelism is necessary
and good and they should be doing it. There is a vast
difference however, between an evangelism sermon and an
evangelistic sermon, between talking about evangelism and
preaching evangelistically. It is possible, of course, to be a
spokesperson for evangelism and an evangelist at the same
time. Why should we not be evangelistic while preaching on
evangelism—or on any other topic, for that matter?

Perhaps the distinction is a matter of degree. Some
sermons obviously fit the description better than others. But
that is not the distinction I have in mind when I speak of
evangelistic preaching. Rather, it is approaching the task of
preaching with evangelistic sensitivity. It is not a particular
type of sermon, and it is certainly not a sermon on the topic
of evangelism. It is recognizing that every sermon must
contain some element of the gospel and appeal for some kind
of response. It is being sensitive, relevant, and understandable to one's hearers. It is showing the personal dimension
of the social gospel and the social implications of the
personal gospel. It is calling for a decision to reaffirm or
reexamine, to profess or confess, to change one's way of
thinking or way of living, to be something greater, or
understand something better, or feel something more deeply.

Evangelistic sensitivity means taking seriously both the
context and the participants in the preaching event. In the
dynamic interaction between the pulpit and the pews something powerful happens when the gospel is faithfully proclaimed, sometimes more in spite of than because of the
eloquence of the preacher. The Holy Spirit can work

miracles even and sometimes especially when we think we have failed miserably, but we owe it to the Spirit who uses us and to the people who hear us to bring our best effort to the task. We make it easier for the Spirit to use us when we relate our message to people's needs in language they can understand, when we identify with them in their struggles and take their questions seriously, and when we preach with conviction and compassion.

To preach with conviction and compassion one must have what John Henry Jowett and many others have called "a passion for souls,"[12] a deep and abiding commitment to help people discover and enter into a saving relationship with Jesus Christ. Jesus "had a passion for saving the lost," wrote Charles Goodell. "No [one] has any right to call himself [or herself] a follower of Jesus who does not share that passion."[13] In another one of his books Goodell repeated this theme: "Before one can preach an evangelistic sermon [one] must have an evangelistic heart."[14] Robert Menzies echoes the sentiment: "Before we engage in this enterprise we must possess as our first requirement a passionate conviction of the superlative importance of the human soul."[15]

"We are called to be guides and guardians of the souls of [persons]," said Jowett in one of his Yale lectures.[16] "Our people must realize that we are bent on serious business, that there is a deep, keen quest in our preaching, a sleepless and a deathless quest. They must feel in the sermon the presence of 'the hound of heaven,' tracking the soul in its most secret ways, following it in the ministry of salvation, to win it from death to life, from life to more abundant life."[17]

"Preach as a dying man to dying men," was Richard Baxter's much-quoted injunction. "We fail them at the very point of their expectations if we fail to feed their souls," warned W. E. Sangster,[18] and George Buttrick declared, "The preacher as a [person] must have faith and passion."[19] Another Lyman Beecher Lecturer at Yale University, Halford Luccock, put it more wryly: "The passion of an evangelist will save the sermon from that last indignity, that of having the deadly drip of a tired commercial."[20]

The point is well made. Where there is no passion, there will be no evangelism. Without passion, a minister is not likely to make the commitment of time and energy that evangelism requires. It would seem that the concern these days is quite the opposite from a passion for saving and serving others. Rather, the concern of many seems to be, How much time must I spend on the job? In the wake of all the concern about pastoral burnout, it is illuminating to read the words of Henry Martyn, who, when he arrived in India as a missionary, wrote in his journal, "I desire to burn out for my God."[21]

What has been said so far and what is to follow applies to preaching generally, which is simply another way of saying that all preaching should be evangelistically sensitive. As pastor-evangelists, we have to approach the task of preaching with the same sensitivity with which we engage in interpersonal evangelism. Before we can do either, we have to be spiritually prepared.

The integrity of preaching is directly related to the integrity of the preacher. A colleague of mine once objected to that assertion. "The gospel has its own integrity," he argued. "It does not depend upon the worthiness of the preacher." My friend's statement is true, but it does not invalidate the assertion. It is not the integrity of the *gospel* that depends upon the integrity of the preacher, but the integrity of the *preaching*. The preacher's words have authority when they are true and consistent with the gospel of Jesus Christ, even if they are uttered by unworthy lips. But the authority of the message and the integrity of the messenger are not the same thing. If we do not believe what we say, then our preaching has no integrity, even if the message is valid. I can say, "Jesus is Lord," but my saying so lacks integrity, if I don't believe it, even though the words are true.

As pastor-evangelists, we of all people should know how vitally important it is that we believe in the Savior in whose name we preach. Can we with integrity exhort others to think and do things that we ourselves do not think or do? As ministers of the gospel of Jesus Christ, can we with integrity be professionals who talk about God but never to God, biblical scholars who can read the scriptures critically but not devotionally, clever pulpiteers who never practice what we preach? Integrity demands that we ourselves know what we believe and why we believe it before we invite others to believe in Christ.

People's hearts are moved much more by conviction than by eloquence. They want to believe that the person speaking to them from the pulpit really believes what she or he is saying. This conviction was reinforced for me by the experience of a brilliant agnostic, who told me that he had walked out in the middle of a sermon during a Christmas Eve service. I suspected that he had had some intellectual problems with the preacher's message, but when I asked him why he had walked out, he replied, "I couldn't bear listening to a man who didn't believe what he was preaching." If a learned agnostic can feel that way, how much more must the average pew sitter!

I have found that to be true also of seminary students, who long for their professors to declare themselves. Students may be impressed by erudition, but they are moved by conviction. They may enjoy theological speculation, but they are inspired by personal affirmation. For men and women whose faith and understanding are being tempered in the crucible of a theological seminary, it is immensely important that their professors speak and act with the integrity of genuine faith as well as with admirable scholarship.

For seminary teachers and preachers alike, the key to integrity is one's devotional life. The pastor-evangelist knows the importance of praying before, during, and after the writing of a sermon and before, during, and after preaching it. Knowing it and doing it are two different things, however. Sometimes, after doing all the research and shuffling through my notes again and again, I find myself sitting there staring at the blank sheet in my typewriter, not knowing where or how to begin. Then I pull away again and pray with a sincerity born of the urgency of my need, and invariably my mental light bulb flashes and I see how to begin. One of my notes jumps out at me, or the perfect opening illustration comes to mind, and my fingers start pounding away at the keys. I confess that sometimes, having just asked for God's help, I incredibly forget to thank God for answering my prayer! But eventually the Spirit prods me to do so, and I'll be thanking God as I type. That's what I mean by praying during, as well as before, the writing of the sermon. It is a constant dialogue with God, whose inspiration we need every minute of the process. God helps us with our writing, and our editing, and our practicing. We need to be as inspired for the second draft as we are for the first, for the Spirit nudges us to use our erasers, too.

No matter what your method of sermon preparation may be, whether you preach from a manuscript, or notes, or memory, the entire process must be undergirded with prayer. If, as Phillips Brooks said, preaching is presenting truth through personality, then sermon preparation has at least as much to do with preparing the preacher as with preparing the sermon. The sermon and the preacher must be inseparably related, and only God can make that happen. If it is going to happen, the Spirit must be present in the pastor's study as well as in the pulpit. After all, the Spirit has many more hours to work with us out of the pulpit than in it.

When you practice your sermons before you preach them, the Holy Spirit is involved in that process too. I find that the more I practice a sermon aloud, the more intensely I begin to feel the message. Far from becoming stale with repetition, a sermon becomes more and more a part of me as I go over it again and again. Even so, there is always a first-time quality about a sermon when I finally preach it from the pulpit. There, too, prayer is the vital link between what is about to happen and all that has led up to it. So before stepping up to the pulpit, we pray that the Holy Spirit will open the hearts and minds of the people and use our words in a powerful way for the glory of God. Even as we preach, we are sending instant prayers to God, and when we finish, we turn the whole event over to God, praying that God will redeem our inadequacies, bless our efforts, and use our words in whatever ways are best for those who heard them.

If we do that, we are less likely to be devastated by criticism, which is the bane of every preacher's existence. Part of our witness to others is the way we respond to our critics, who can always find something in our sermons with which to disagree. The pastor-evangelist sees a reasonable critic not as an enemy but as a potential friend, someone whose criticism, if listened to appreciatively and not defensively, can be turned into a compliment. But that, unfortunately, is easier said then done. The temptation is to defend ourselves, a tactic that never seems to work. "Never explain yourself," my father used to say. "Your friends don't need it, and your critics won't believe it." That is good advice for us preachers, who should know as well as anyone that vindication belongs to God. We can trust that in God's time and in God's way we shall be able to look back with the hindsight of faith and see that in everything God is working for good.

When we consign the results of our preaching efforts to the Holy Spirit, we also relieve ourselves of the burden of thinking it all depends on us. How soon we otherwise grow weary from the weight of indispensability. It is not that we can excuse ourselves from doing the very best we can. There is a big difference between depending on and presuming upon God. But we can preach with the assurance that God can work wonders in and through us, when we strive to be faithful. We cannot, nor should we, guarantee that everyone in the congregation will like our sermons. But we can and we should promise that what we preach will be biblically based, theologically sound, carefully prepared, and existentially relevant. If we keep our promise, praying for God's help all along the way, our preaching will have integrity. But that is a big "if," and we need to examine what keeping that promise entails.

8

Planning
the Preaching

Prayer can give integrity to our words, but we owe God
and our hearers more than that. When we pray as if it all
depends on God and prepare as if it all depends on us, we
bring God not a thimble but a basket to fill. As pastor-
evangelists, we must use our best skills and wisdom in our
preaching ministry. "The wise minister preaches according
to a program," said Andrew Blackwood many years ago.[22]
Whether we are called to preach every Sunday, or twice a
month, or only occasionally, we need to *plan*. Incidentally,
if you are one who preaches only at the invitation of a senior
minister or head of staff, you have a right to know how often
and when you will preach, so that you *can* plan. You need
to consider the when, where, why, and what of the situation,
so that your sermons, ideally, can maintain the continuity of
the preaching ministry while establishing a continuity of their
own. You may be preaching for four Sundays in a row while
your colleague is on vacation, for example, in which case
you could do a series of sermons, each one relating to some
unifying theme but having its own message for the people
who were not there for the other sermons.

Or you may be preaching with large time intervals between
your pulpit appearances. That being the case, you may want
to consider a nonconsecutive series, in which each succeed-
ing sermon would have some relationship or reference to the
ones that preceded it, simply to give continuity and movement to your own preaching. At the same time you would,
of course, keep in mind all the other factors that determine
the theme of a worship service, such as the Christian year,

special Sundays, and the other considerations discussed in chapter 2. Sermon series have a positive evangelistic effect, for they arouse the interest of visitors and members alike, provided your theme is interesting.

The Sermon Schedule

Whether or not you use a lectionary, much benefit is to be gained from planning your preaching well in advance, preferably a year. (See Appendix E for an example of how to set up a worship schedule.) A well-planned sermon schedule offers many advantages.

Planning is a time-saver. You spend far more time when you plan only from one Sunday to the next. The selection of sermon topics alone takes much longer that way. You might have a terrible time deciding which of five likely subjects should be the one for next Sunday, whereas if you are planning for a whole year, you can decide how you can best work all five of them into the schedule. By the time you finish your schedule for the year, you are usually well into the next year's schedule, and even beyond that. The Lenten sermon series that you don't use one year can be used the next. It also saves preparation time, for when you know what you are going to be preaching about in the coming months, you have a place to file the sermon illustrations and other thoughts that come to you along the way. For every sermon I am planning to preach, I have a working file for such items. When the time comes to prepare a particular sermon, I am way ahead of where I would be if I were starting "from scratch."

Planning permits flexibility. You are less likely to fall into ruts, when you plan ahead. You can build into your schedule a variety of preaching styles and sermon types. At the same time, planning ahead does not restrict you from departing from the schedule on any given Sunday. I have said that the sermon I preached the Sunday following the assassination of President Kennedy was not the one I had planned. As it happened to be Thanksgiving Sunday, my new topic was

"Thanksgiving in a Time of Tragedy." So, too, when some other event of world-shaking significance occurs, one is free to adjust accordingly. Furthermore, even though the subjects have been planned in advance, the sermons are not written until the week before they are preached, so that it is possible to be as up to date with the news as one wants to be.

Planning encourages breadth and depth. By planning ahead, you can force yourself to preach on texts and topics that challenge you, or that you have neglected, or that stretch you and your congregation biblically and theologically. You work harder at presenting the full gospel rather than dwelling on your own pet themes. As you look over your yearly sermon schedules, you can tell very easily which doctrinal and topical themes you need to address or from which books of the Bible you need to preach.

Planning facilitates coordination. There are a number of persons who would appreciate having a copy of your sermon schedule containing the scripture lessons, hymns, responsive readings, and other pertinent information. The music director, if you have one, will be delighted to have your sermon topics a year in advance. Then she or he many times (not necessarily every Sunday) can plan special music to coordinate with your message. How grateful I was to work with a music director who, after receiving my schedule, would provide me with a similar schedule of the special music for the coming year, so that I could refer to the texts for illustrative purposes, when they were particularly appropriate to the theme. That kind of coordination is a most valuable aid to the unity of a worship service.

The editor of your church newsletter, if you have one, also will appreciate having the sermon topics and texts in advance, for publicity purposes. The sexton, if there is one, will be glad to know next Sunday's sermon title, so that it can be posted on the outdoor bulletin board. Most important of all, you will be able to select the hymns that best fit the theme of the service for every Sunday of the year, while covering a much wider selection than you are likely to otherwise. When you choose them Sunday by Sunday, you often find yourself wishing you had used a particular hymn with this sermon instead of that one, or you tend to use some hymns much more frequently than perhaps you should.

Planning stimulates congregational participation. Announcing what you will be preaching on in the coming weeks and what the scripture passages will be enables people to read and meditate on the appropriate passages for the coming Sunday. Such preparation makes the worship experience all the more meaningful for both you and the congregation.

Planning promotes interest. Members as well as visitors appreciate your planning. It excites their interest and encourages their regular attendance, as they get caught up in the continuity of your preaching ministry. Many discover for the first time that the gospel is a many-faceted jewel which those who worship only sporadically can never fully appreciate. The sermon they miss may be the very one they needed most to hear. As they look over the sermon topics listed in the bulletin for the coming weeks, they find themselves not wanting to miss any of them. You will find more and more people wanting printed copies of the sermons they missed, as well as the sermons they heard.

Planning expedites retrieval. After several years of preaching, you will have hundreds of sermons in your barrel. Sometimes you will want to take a fresh look at a topic or text on which you know you have preached before. Your sermon schedules serve as a chronological index, through which you can thumb more quickly and easily than you can your manuscripts. This is especially helpful when you are thinking about using a sermon you have preached before and want to scan your schedules for ideas. You can do that even more efficiently when your sermons are cross-indexed by topic and text. That might be a good project for an eager volunteer who would like to be helpful.

Sermon Ideas

The frustration of most preachers is not the paucity of their ideas but the abundance of them.[23] When I graduated from seminary I had already accumulated a file of hundreds of sermon ideas, many of them with skeleton outlines. If I had never had another idea, I had enough to last me for twenty years of preaching. The file increased day by day, until I no longer kept count. What I soon discovered was that I would never be able to preach all the sermons I would like to preach. If I could live to be a thousand, I could never exhaust the store of sermon ideas begging to be preached. I do not know many preachers who wouldn't say the same thing. That being the case, it behooves us to choose our texts and topics wisely. If we can't say everything, we ought to have good reasons for what we do say, and what we say ought to be important.

Whence cometh our ideas? From many sources, obviously, but for me they come mostly from my devotional reading of the scriptures. The Bible continues to speak so relevantly and contemporaneously to every aspect of life that I find myself adding new sermon ideas to my file every time I read even the most familiar texts. New insights, new twists, new applications jump out at me as I read and meditate on whatever passage it happens to be. Sometimes the whole outline for a sermon opens up and I hurriedly scribble the thoughts on a card or a piece of paper, lest I fail to recapture them later. Sermon ideas come from many other sources, too, and at any time of the day or night. Sometimes the best ideas come before I'm fully awake, and I've had to learn in my semiconscious state to force myself to get up and write them down before they slip out of the grasp of my memory.

The best way to file sermon ideas is probably not the most feasible way. If preaching were all you had to do, you could spend the time needed to cross-index your ideas by topic and text, but most pastors are far too busy to justify that kind of time. I have lists of sermon ideas under various themes and types of service—ideas for communion meditations, the seasons of the Christian year, doctrinal themes, stewardship sermons, and so on. Many of the ideas are written in the margins of Bibles I have used over the years, and there are thick files of ideas for sermons that don't fit under any particular category. The planning process for me has always begun with my wading through my lists and files. It's a most exciting and enjoyable undertaking, in which the Holy Spirit is very much involved. New ideas come in the very act of sorting through other ideas; it's a dynamic process.

There is, to be sure, a long way to go from an idea to the finished sermon. Although I think topically, I develop an idea biblically. That too is a dynamic process, as the Bible often sends me off in a quite different direction from that which I had originally anticipated. Sermon ideas should always be open-ended, until the Holy Spirit gives them form and shape through the scriptures. As we undergird the entire creative enterprise with prayer, the Spirit intercedes for us and enables us to think the thoughts God puts into our minds and hearts. That does not discount the importance of our own serious exegetical work, thorough research, thoughtful selection of illustrations, prudent decisions regarding the approach and style, and careful writing.

The Sermon Title

Donald Macleod used to ask the students in his preaching class whether their sermon topic would induce Sadie Glutz to get off the bus and go to church. It is incredible to me that some of the best preachers I know can come up with the most pedantic, unimaginative sermon titles. They can hardly be thinking evangelistically when they announce a title such as "The Ecological Crisis from a Theological Perspective." Why not "Who Owns the Universe?" I doubt if Sadie would get off the bus to go hear a sermon on "Seven Traditional Theories of the Atonement," but she might want to know "Why Jesus Died."

Many travelers and church shoppers decide where they will worship on a given Sunday on the basis of a sermon title that catches their attention in the church advertisement section of the local Saturday newspaper. You may have prepared a great sermon for that Sunday, but would anyone guess it from seeing the title in the newspaper, or on the church sign, or in the church bulletin? Let's face it: church members look at sermon topics too, especially people for whom the preaching of the Word is a significant part of worship.

What is a good sermon title? It is one that evokes interest, arouses curiosity, and invites people to come hear what you have to say. The best titles are the ones to which people can relate personally rather than abstractly. "How to Be Happy" will grab their attention more quickly than "The Doctrine of Christian Contentment."

A sermon title should not be too long. As a general rule, it should have no more than seven words, and the longer the words the fewer there should be. The title should be interesting but not gimmicky; it goes without saying that it should not be offensive, crass, or crude. Most important, it should be clearly related to the theme of the sermon. People can be surprised, but they should never feel deceived by the title. It might not tell them for sure what the sermon is about, but after hearing the sermon, they should know why the title was chosen. The evangelistic moral of all this is, Give particular attention to the title of your sermon!

Sermon Illustrations

I am a little intimidated by some of the things some writers have to say on this subject. The elaborate filing system they recommend would take a busy pastor far more time than she or he could afford to spend, just to file illustrations, let alone find them. There is no denying the importance of apt illustrations for good preaching, and no escaping the need for some systematic way of storing and recalling them. Whether you use a computer for that purpose or do it the old-fashioned way, with scores of manila folders arranged alphabetically by topic in a filing cabinet, it is an endless task.

Over the years I have accumulated three file drawers of sermon illustrations, but I have found myself resorting to the material in those files less and less as the years go by. There are three main reasons for that decline.

1. The first and most important reason is that because I plan ahead, I am able to file the illustrations with a particular sermon. This practice has resulted in my not having to add as many new illustrations to the general file, although I continue to add some and I have not entirely stopped using those files.

2. The second reason is that I use illustrations rather sparingly and selectively, and the ones I do use are more often drawn from the immediate circumstances and experiences of life. Instead of collecting illustrations that I may use *sometime,* I tend to find those which relate to a particular topic or theme I'll be preaching on in the next year or two. That's far enough ahead for me, and I'm thankful to be relieved of the burdensome chore of classifying, filing, and cross-indexing scads of illustrations I may never use.

3. A third reason for not using my illustration file as much as I used to has to do with my own writing and preaching style. I'd rather find a colorful way to say something than quote someone else. I'd rather my sermon be original than second-hand, and I'd rather listen to one that is original. But that is my peculiar predilection. I certainly do not fault anyone who feels otherwise, and I greatly admire those masters of the art of illustration whose range of selectivity is mind-boggling.

One of my favorite means of what I call productive relaxation is writing poetry. It is also an outlet for creative expression, which I often incorporate into my sermon writing. Sometimes my pulpit rhymes are intended to convey a truth in a humorous way, as was the following verse used in a sermon on financial stewardship:

> A trip to Hawaii for me and my spouse,
>   A new motorbike for young Tod,
> The dentist says braces for Sally and Jane,
>   So what does that leave for God?

A sum set aside for the kids' college years,
    Plus payments on Timmy's hot rod,
Repairs on the house, entertainment and food,
    How much does that leave for God?

I stand for the unity taught by the church,
    I give it much more than a nod:
One faith, and one hope, and one baptism, *and*
    One dollar a week for God!

More often the verses are in a serious vein, such as the following poem based on Isaiah 6:1–8, written to be used in an ordination or installation sermon:

No vision of the King of kings,
    No holy trains, no seraph wings,
No throne of glory have I seen,
    So who am I with lips unclean,
Amid these people born to dwell,
    God's word to speak, God's truth to tell?

No altar, with a burning coal
    To touch my lips and cleanse my soul,
No thund'rous antiphons proclaim
    To all on earth God's holy name,
No shaking temple filled with smoke,
    No voice that to Isaiah spoke.

No prophet's thoughts my mind have crossed,
    Save "Woe is me, for I am lost!"
Yet is it not God's voice I hear
    Within my heart? The call is clear:
"Whom shall I send for us this day?"
    Lord, here am I. Send me, I pray!

We have been reminded often enough not to downplay the educative value of storytelling. It is probably true that most people remember stories better than they recall propositions. The use of narrative has even been given a theological justification, for which there is a solid biblical basis. Even so, there are two words of caution to the pastor-evangelist regarding the use of illustrations. One is not to let the illustrative tale wag the sermonic dog. Illustrations are a means to an end, not an end in themselves. They should do what their name implies—illustrate. The other word of caution is to make sure that the illustrations you choose will communicate to your hearers. Be sensitive to the visitors and others in the congregation who may not be familiar with your biblical references, or understand your literary quotations, or respond to your in-house humor.

The Sermon Manuscript

Is there to be or not to be a manuscript, that is also the question! The controversy is greater regarding its use in the pulpit than about the value of writing it, although opinion is divided even with regard to the latter. Once again, my intention is to examine the question from an evangelistic perspective, and I find myself aligned with those who advocate the weekly discipline of writing out their sermons. I admit there have been times when I was tempted to bypass the rigorous demands which the production of a manuscript imposed on my time. It is so much easier to have a simple outline of my main points and a general idea of what I want to say, and not worry so much about how to say it when the time comes. After many years of writing out my sermons, however, the discipline has become habitual, to the extent that now I can't go to bed on Saturday night until the manuscript is finished.

Saturday night? Yes, that's an admission that some weeks I've been caught with my sermon down. Every pastor has experienced those weeks when a combination of circumstances completely consumed the normal sermon-writing time. Then, if ever, one might excuse oneself from the chore of writing a manuscript, but somehow my homiletical conscience won't let me do that, probably because it knows that I could easily learn to rationalize myself out of the habit. It would be disastrous to make a practice of writing your Sunday sermon on Saturday night, and for me impossible if I had to start from scratch. Working with a sermon schedule has saved me from the calamity, inasmuch as I have known and thought about the topic off and on for weeks or months in advance.

One of the main reasons for writing out your sermons in advance has evangelistic import. The written sermon can be reproduced and made available to shut-ins, out-of-towners, people who were not in church that day, and whoever else is interested. Your written sermons can thus become an important evangelistic aid, as members of the congregation share them with friends, relatives, and neighbors.

The reproduction process, by the way, is much easier with a manuscript than without one. It is much more laborious and time-consuming to transcribe the sermon from a cassette tape, which does not have the benefit of paragraphing and punctuation. The result of the latter method, moreover, is likely to be far less satisfactory, as the written version will reveal all the flaws and defects of normal conversational speech. To avoid that problem, the first typed draft of the tape will have to be carefully edited and perhaps largely rewritten, thus adding to the tediousness of the process. A written transcript of what is said in some pulpits would be an embarrassment to the preacher. If there are facilities for reproducing the cassettes, it might be safer to make them available, in addition to or in lieu of written copies.

The discipline of writing your sermons in advance minimizes sloppy or shallow thinking and maximizes clarity and sharpness. This is especially important if yours are teaching sermons, in which you prefer to pack solid content rather than froth. If you want your hearers to think, they deserve to hear something you have thought about and prepared well. You have time in your study to give the topic your best thought, to search for the best ways of expressing your ideas, and to present your thoughts in the most logical and convincing order. You can, furthermore, reduce the risk of the unhelpful digressions and unnecessary verbiage that characterize the sermons of some preachers who scoff at the idea of a manuscript.

Your sermon manuscripts can be filed for future revision and use. Some ministers believe their sermons should not be preached more than once. They may be right! My own feeling, however, is that most pastors have more than a few sermons that are worth preaching again. That is the salvation of many guest preachers, who do not have time to write a new sermon every time they are invited to preach. That does not mean they put no thought or effort into their preparation. No sermon of mine is ever exactly the same the next time it is preached. It is always updated and applied to the new situation. Sometimes it is changed completely.

My sermons may be of no monetary value, but I look upon them as my most precious possession. They represent hours and hours and hours of time and energy and agonizing. They are the product of my sincerest thoughts, my deepest faith, my noblest aspirations. They are a record of my theological development, my ongoing spiritual pilgrimage, my progressive struggle to understand and apply the gospel. They are who I was and who I am. There are times when I need to go back and see what I had to say on a particular issue or subject before tackling it again. I could not do that if I had no record of what I said.

A sermon file is useful and important for more than just personal reasons. It is one more resource upon which you can draw when you want to give a person something helpful to read. I've often had occasion to pull a sermon out of the file and copy it for someone. That too is an evangelistic advantage of having such a file.

For some ministers the most important reason for writing out their sermons is that they preach from a manuscript. Everyone has his or her own preaching style. The question is not whether it is best to preach from a manuscript, from notes, or from memory, but what is the best method for *you*. It is not automatically the case that preachers always choose the method that best suits their individual style. Some who don't use a manuscript would be more effective if they did, and some who do would be better off if they did not. The goal is communication. If the manuscript gets in the way, you probably should try preaching from notes. If you are not very fluent or good at extemporizing or memorizing, you might try using a manuscript.

Using a manuscript does not necessarily mean reading it. It is possible to use a manuscript without hampering eye contact or impairing communication. I *preach* from a manuscript but *speak* and *teach* extemporaneously or from notes, depending upon the situation and the assignment. As a preacher, my method of preparation is to go over my sermon orally as many times as I can, until I know it well, without having put myself through the strain of trying to memorize it. In the pulpit, the manuscript is then so familiar to me that one glance recalls half a page or more. For me, it is like preaching from notes, only better, for I have thought long and hard about how I am going to say what I have to say. For that reason I don't want to say it differently in the pulpit.

At the same time I must quickly add that I never feel bound to the manuscript. The Holy Spirit is free to prompt me as I speak; I just hope it is the Holy Spirit doing the prompting! The manuscript is more like a tether than a straitjacket. It allows me plenty of room to roam, if the Spirit moves me.

The secret of preaching from a manuscript is only partly in the delivery. Granted, it is an important part, but equally important is the manuscript itself. It must be written to be spoken. That requires the skill of knowing how to write in a conversational style. It must not sound like a doctoral thesis or a term paper. Writing something that is to be spoken does not mean forsaking all rules of syntax and grammar. Conversational writing can also be good writing. Indeed, the double test of good sermon writing is whether or not the sermon reads as well as it preaches and preaches as well as it reads. How do you accomplish that? By going over the sermon aloud again and again, each time modifying the wording and phrasing until what you have written feels natural and comfortable when you say it. I find myself making little changes almost every time I preach or read through a sermon. It is never exactly the same as it is written. The Holy Spirit is constantly at work.

For me, sermon writing is an enjoyable but not an easy task. The total amount of time it takes to prepare a sermon is difficult if not impossible to measure. One would have to assign to each sermon a portion of the time spent planning the worship and preaching schedule, plus time for all the brooding, praying, and reflecting one spends over and above the research and writing time. When it comes to the actual sermon, I can spend an hour or more on a single sentence or even a phrase. As I have already mentioned I sit and stare at the keyboard for a couple of hours, waiting for the inspiration to begin. That's the time I am trying to decide what approach to take. What is the best vehicle for this particular message? Should it be in the style of a first-person sermon, a narrative, a dialogue? Should I start with an illustration, a quotation, a repetition of the text, a question, an affirmation, an assertion? These are the kinds of thoughts with which my brain has to grapple as I turn to the task of writing.

In their younger years my children had to learn that this was not the time to disturb Daddy. It took them a while to understand that if they saw me doing nothing, it didn't mean I wasn't doing anything! They would peek into my study and see me staring at the keyboard "doing nothing" and assume that was a good time to come with whatever complaint or greeting or bit of news they wanted to share. Every such interruption during that staring period was disastrous to my thought process, and afterward I would have to gear up all over again.

Once I begin to write I go at an average rate of about two hours per double-spaced typewritten page. Now I use a word processor for my creative writing. When I was using a typewriter, the first draft was always full of deletions and insertions but was basically the way I wanted it. From then on, there would be minor additions and corrections but usually no major changes, just refinements. Having revised the first draft sufficiently to my liking, I then retype the sermon single-spaced on two 8½-by-11-inch sheets of paper folded in half and stapled in the middle to form a little booklet. This is the manuscript I use for practicing, for preaching, and for filing. It has the advantage of taking only two sheets' worth of space in the file drawer, as it is placed in the folder in an open position. It is also easier for me to handle in the pulpit.

On the front page of each sermon booklet is listed the sermon index number, series number (if applicable), the topic, text, scripture lessons, hymns used on the day it was preached, resources and references consulted and used, the date and place it was preached, and other pertinent information, such as references to related sermons and subsequent dates it is preached. I keep the original drafts and the finished manuscripts in two different places, so that in the event of a fire in one place, there will still be another copy. Some are now stored on disks.

The Use of the Bible

"I'm a biblical preacher," declared one minister in a recent workshop. "With a bit of skillful eisegesis I can make most any text fit what I want to say!" The comment drew a loud laugh from the other persons present. The trouble was, however, that the person who made the comment was dead serious.

I consider myself a biblical preacher too, but that is not the approach I have in mind. It is not a matter of imposing my thinking on a text but of letting the text inform my thinking. Another way to say it is that I think topically but I develop a topic biblically. Regardless of how one might classify a particular sermon, be it textual, topical, expository, or whatever, in any case let it be biblical.

It is possible, for example, to distinguish between an expository sermon, which attempts to expound and apply a particular passage of scripture, of whatever length, and a topical sermon, which attempts to develop a particular theme, subject, or idea, using appropriate scriptural references. Both represent biblical preaching, although the focus is different. One centers on the passage; the other centers on a topic, such as faith, prayer, Mary Magdalene, eternal life, stewardship, or the Christian attitude toward war. The development of a topical sermon can cause one to draw from many different parts of the Bible. The distinction between the two basic types of sermons is blurred when a preacher does an exposition of a particular passage to see what light it sheds on a particular topic. An exposition of 2 Corinthians 8:1–15 would be an excellent way to address the topic of financial stewardship, for example.

Some ministers have either forgotten or have never discovered the importance and value of biblical preaching. The Bible is the basic source of our knowledge of God and of Jesus Christ. It gives authority and power to our message. It is the richest treasure of sermon ideas and illustrations. For every human situation and condition, the Bible has a word as timely and relevant as the morning newscast. It is an inspiring book because it is an inspired book, whose central figure throughout is God. For that reason, it is a divine book, but it is also an intensely human book, which both reflects the heights and exposes the depths of human nature. The saying is true: "Most books inform, a few reform, the Bible alone transforms."[24] To neglect, minimize, or downplay the Bible in our preaching is not only a tragic mistake but a reprehensible dereliction of duty. We owe it to our hearers and to God to be biblical preachers. How can a pastor-evangelist be anything else?

The Sermon Content

I have served as a reference for many a minister friend whom I have never heard preach. When a representative of the pastor nominating committee asks me about such a person's ability in the pulpit, I can only speculate about the quality of the preaching, based on my knowledge of the quality of the person. My estimate will be formed partly by the person's writing ability; if I've seen some sermon manuscripts, so much the better. Then I can comment on the quality of the content. Good preaching begins not in the pulpit but in the study, where the content of a sermon is determined. We shall examine this subject more thoroughly in chapter 10, where we shall try to answer the question, What exactly is an evangelistic sermon?

But first there are some things that need to be said of a more general nature about evangelistic preaching.

9

Preaching
the Sermon

At the beginning of chapter 7, I described what I mean by evangelistic preaching. For me, it means preaching with evangelistic sensitivity to both content and delivery. It manifestly has much to do with the content of the message, to which subject we shall turn in the next chapter. It also has to do with the delivery and other related factors, which should not be divorced from the content but which for purposes of discussion can be considered separately.

Of all the good books I have read on the subject of preaching, the most complete, practical, and helpful for me was George Sweazey's excellent book *Preaching the Good News*. The title could be a definition of evangelistic preaching, yet Dr. Sweazey includes a three-page section on the specific topic of evangelistic preaching, in contradistinction to other kinds.[25] The distinction illustrates my earlier point that most of what the authorities have to say about preaching in general would be applicable to evangelistic preaching. Nevertheless, a valid distinction needs to be made. Having already described that distinction very briefly in chapter 7, I want to return to it now and take a closer look at the distinguishing characteristics of evangelistic preaching. Since what holds true for preaching in general is also true for evangelistic preaching in particular, it can be said fairly that the distinction between the general and the particular usually is a matter of degree, but that degree is significant enough to be distinguishable and distinguishable enough to be discussed.

The Preacher's Awareness

Evangelistic sensitivity means being aware of the people in the pews. The pastor-evangelist is more conscious than some preachers appear to be of the evangelistic challenge that every congregation represents. It is as true of our parishioners as it is of the unchurched strangers who wander in that everyone has questions and doubts, problems and needs, fears and anxieties, pains and sorrows, hopes and dreams. The evangelistic preacher takes seriously the agnostic in us all, the seeker, the sufferer, the sinner in us all. The doubts, the fears, the guilt, the pain may be acknowledged or unacknowledged, identified or unidentified, confessed or unconfessed by the people to whom we preach, but they exist to some degree in everyone.

The pastor-evangelist knows that in every congregation there are persons whose faith needs to be reaffirmed or reconfirmed, encouraged or challenged, renewed or revitalized, enlightened or enlisted, nurtured or nourished, reinspired or reinforced. It is not as if everyone is on the same rung of the ladder of faith, not to mention the differences in age, health, race, nationality, vocabulary, personality, character, habits, hobbies, talents, interests, values, morals, sexual orientation, intellectual capacity, educational background, family status, social position, income level, religious experience, political viewpoint, mental attitude, and degree of motivation, to name a few. What a tremendous challenge to the preacher, whose task it is to preach a sermon that is relevant to such a heterogeneous gathering!

To the unchurched in the congregation, the preacher must be an evangelist. For those who are already members of the church, the task is renewal and the preacher literally speaking is more of a revivalist. Both groups need to hear the gospel, but their different relationships to the church call for differences in the preacher's appeal for decision. Evangelism and revivalism are related but different, and the pastor-evangelist is sensitive to the differences as well as the similarities. The pastor-evangelist as preacher is therefore both an evangelist and a revivalist, always striving to communicate to the unchurched as well as to the flock.

The communication theorists have been helpful in identifying and labeling the various stages of the communication process and the factors that affect it.[26] Those who have diagnosed and described this fascinating phenomenon have developed a technical language for describing what communication practitioners have known to be true for a long time: that communication is a two-way street in which both the sender and the receiver have a role. Applying that truth to the preaching event, we can say that communication depends as much on the hearer as on the preacher. We didn't need the theorists to tell us that, but it is worth remembering, for congregations have to be taught how to listen to sermons as much as preachers need to learn how to deliver them.

Part of a preacher's awareness is that "sense of the occasion" referred to earlier in connection with the pastor-evangelist's role as worship leader. In the pulpit, in front of the altar, or behind the communion table, the pastor-evangelist needs to be on top of the situation. That means being able to respond to the unexpected and able to say the right thing at the right time. Every preacher has to deal with interruptions in the pulpit, such as the time our public-address system picked up a shortwave radio conversation between two truck drivers. Had I ignored the interruption, all communication would have ceased. A humorous comment to the effect that the voice we were hearing was not the Lord's relieved the tension, the problem was soon solved, and we returned to the subject.

On one occasion the guest preacher in a university chapel was preaching on the topic "Walking About Zion" (Ps. 48:12). We had heard the phrase many times, when halfway through the sermon a young protester clad only in sneakers, shorts, and a T-shirt appeared in the back of the chapel and proceeded down the long center aisle, up into the chancel, back down one side aisle, up the center and into the chancel again, and back down the other side. He didn't say a word,

but he sure captured the attention of every person there—
except the preacher, who went merrily on, trying to ignore
this wild-haired figure parading in front of him, round and
round the sanctuary. All communication had ceased between the pulpit and the pews. Everyone was waiting for
someone else to do something, but nobody did anything,
until after about five minutes the campus security guards
arrived and apprehended the culprit as he rounded the rear
pew for the fourth time. Still nothing was said from the
pulpit, and who knows what the poor fellow had been talking
about for the last five minutes. Everyone was concerned and
sympathetic, but no one was listening. Yet all he would have
had to do was thank the young man for providing a live
illustration of the text, for there he was, walking about Zion!
The humor would have shown the congregation that the
preacher was on top of the situation, and the escapade would
have ended much sooner. The moral of the story is, Never
ignore an unexpected interruption.

A sense of the occasion also means being aware of those
others who have spoken before you or will speak after you
and being gracious and inclusive in your references and
remarks. Too many preachers act as if they are the only
persons who have anything to contribute to the edification of
the congregation. The pastor-evangelist knows how to present others in the best light to assure their being received in
the best spirit, how to call attention to the valuable lessons
of another person's life or words, and how to help people
recognize and appreciate the value of what they are expe-
riencing. It is all part of the characteristic that I call
awareness.

The Preacher's Style

To paraphrase the words of a song that was popular a
generation or so ago, "It ain't what you say, it's the way that
you say it. That's what gets results!" To the extent that
communication between the pulpit and the pew depends on
the preacher, one crucial determinant is the preacher's style

I use that word to include several characteristics that distinguish, or should distinguish, evangelistic preaching.

Authenticity. The importance of the preacher's integrity needs to be reemphasized at this point. The best advice to any preacher is, Be yourself! Don't be one person in the pulpit and a different person out of it. People will not listen to phonies. Preachers who assume airs in the pulpit receive cold stares from the pews. Why does God have to be pronounced Gawd in the pulpit? And why does the Spirit have to become the Spidit? We preachers have enough trouble with the unfavorable images some people have of us without giving them additional cause. The fact that genuineness is indispensable to evangelistic preaching is consistent with communication theory, which declares that the character of the sender is crucial to the receptivity of the receiver.

Clarity. The pastor-evangelist as preacher strives hard to be clear, knowing that clarity is essential to understanding. That too is a challenge, given the diversity of our hearers. It requires a constant self-monitoring of our preacher talk, to make sure we are not talking only to ourselves. "Simple speech," said Martin Luther in one of his "Table Talks" on the subject of preaching, "is the best and truest eloquence." That does not mean we have to discard all theological language and the great doctrinal terms, like salvation, justification, redemption, gospel, sin, and grace. What it means is that we should not assume, when we do use such terms, that our hearers understand them. Rather, we should define, explain, and illustrate words that may not be understandable to everyone in the congregation. We should, as Luther advised, "instruct the common people." Today we would say "the average church member." The hope is that in this way the congregation will become familiar and comfortable with the terms.

Variety. Because of the diversity of the people in the pews, the pastor-evangelist will want to vary the approach, hoping in that way to reach everyone at some time or another. The decision will be partly determined by the emphasis of the sermon. Is it primarily motivational or informational? Is it inspirational or educational? Does it call for an exhortative or a reflective style? Is the mood prophetic or pastoral? Does it stress the social or the personal gospel? Does it have a corporate or an individual thrust? It may reflect many of these emphases at once or alternately, and the preacher's delivery will reflect whatever the mood. Variety—of pitch, pace, intensity, inflection, and volume—reduces the risk of monotony.

Varying the approach avoids the danger of monotony and keeps people mentally alert and ready for surprises. As the saying goes, "Variety is the spice of life." A first-person sermon can be an exciting departure from one's normal approach, provided it is thoughtfully prepared and well delivered. A major pitfall for preachers who attempt first-person sermons is failing to establish a tenable rationale and a plausible context for the person whose identity you have assumed to be there. You can set the stage before the sermon with a brief word of explanation during the announcements or by a notice in the church bulletin. I almost always prefer, however, to allow the congregation to make the discovery at the start of the sermon itself. The congregation, in a sense, is part of the role-play, and if you are assuming the identity of another person, you have to establish a conceivable reason for that person to be addressing them. You can do this by addressing the congregation directly. For example: "Greetings in the name of our Lord Jesus Christ! Although you have read my letters, you have never seen me in the flesh. My name is Paul, and I am here this morning to speak to you on a most important aspect of our faith and life."

In some first-person sermons you will not be speaking directly to the congregation. If that is the case, you will have to convey the idea clearly that the congregation is listening in on the character's musings or conversation with someone else. One advantage of this approach is something I learned when I was in advertising: People tend to listen more carefully to what they overhear than to what they hear. They concentrate better when they are eavesdropping than when they are being spoken to directly. For an example of the latter type of first-person sermon, see Appendix F.

Another major pitfall is that of failing to present a message that is logically consistent with the established context. If you are the apostle Paul, remember how you got there and why, so that your conclusion is powerfully coherent. Your message must conform completely to Paul's theology and style. You have to get yourself out of it and actually "become" Paul. Only then will it be believable and persuasive.

Interest. Variety raises the interest rate. It goes without saying that an evangelistic preacher should be an interesting speaker. The content can be excellent, but if there is no spark in the preacher, the sermon will ignite no fires in the pews. Many people will simply stop listening. To be dull is deadly. If the preacher is not alive and excited about the sermon, it is hardly likely that the congregation will be. The story is told of the man who dreamed he was preaching a sermon, and when he woke up, he was! But the congregation was still asleep. Variety of approach, creativity of expression, and timely topics with relevant illustrations all help to stimulate interest, but what helps more than anything else is the personality of the preacher. If the preacher is an interesting person, the listeners will be interested. It's as simple as that.

Warmth. In line with what has already been said, a cold personality is a serious detriment to evangelism. A warm preacher makes a warm congregation. The friendliness that every church would like to be known for begins in the pulpit. Warmth calls for a relational, dialogical, and personal style of preaching. It is a high compliment when people say, "You were speaking right to me today, Pastor!" In preaching, as in interpersonal evangelism, you can say the hard thing if your facial expressions and body language convey the warmth and love of a caring pastor. A scowl does not communicate joy, and a clenched fist and tight jaws belie one's verbal expressions of love. The best clue as to how you are coming across in your preaching is whether people are coming to you with their problems. They are not likely to seek the help of someone they perceive to be austere, aloof, and judgmental. For most people, an unsympathetic preacher in the pulpit means an unapproachable pastor in the study. The pastor-evangelist identifies with the persons in the pews, talking *to* them (not *at* them), thinking *with* them (not *for* them), empathizing (not criticizing), helping (not haranguing), inviting (not coercing), challenging (not threatening). Style is a product of personality. A warm personality is not something one turns on and off to suit the occasion. It must be genuine and natural, not superficial and artificial. It is an expression of one's heart. In short, a pastor-evangelist is a "people person," someone who really loves people.

Consistency. As a preacher, the pastor-evangelist is especially sensitive to the need for logical consistency. You and I are apologists as well as evangelists, persuaders as well as proclaimers. We have to be aware of the assumptions that underlie our preaching, and we have to confess them and communicate them to our hearers. These are the givens of our faith, our theological presuppositions, which are not self-evidently true to people who do not share them. Whether our hearers agree with them or not, it is nonetheless essential that our case be consistent with our assumptions— or, to put it in clergy jargon, that our evangelistic methodology be consistent with our theological presuppositions. One does not worry so much about that when one is not thinking evangelistically. So many sermons are replete with dogmatic assertions, spoken not as affirmations of faith but as self-evident truths. It is much easier to proclaim than to persuade. Unprovable pulpit pronouncements may impress gullible believers, but they are not likely to convince discerning questioners. To be sure, there are times for proclamation and for declaration, but we must always be aware of our need to make the case, to be advocates for Jesus Christ. If we don't, who will? If we can't, who can?

Expectancy. Evangelistic preaching is optimistic. There is an expectancy about it, born not of a naïve self-confidence but of the preacher's trust in the presence and power of the Holy Spirit. Evangelistic preaching blends expectancy with a humility that is content to leave the results to God. The reluctance of some preachers to ask for any kind of response at the end of their sermons may be due less to their theological reservations than to their spiritual expectations. "I can't imagine the sophisticated people I preach to ever responding to an altar call," objected one minister rather indignantly and conclusively, when that suggestion was made by another minister at a clergy gathering. "Have you ever tried it?" asked the friend. "No, and I never will," replied the first minister vehemently. "Then how can you be sure no one ever would respond?" That is precisely the point. Expect nothing, receive nothing. Expect results, and receive the miracles of God's grace.

Urgency. One characteristic of evangelistic preaching in which it differs in degree most clearly from preaching in general is the urgency of its appeal. Some call it "preaching for a verdict." I have never been comfortable with that expression—it connotes the limited alternatives of the courtroom: "Guilty" or "Not guilty." Is that the only choice we want to offer people? To be sure, an evangelistic sermon calls for a response from the hearer. It has a once-for-all, now-or-never, all-or-nothing, either-or quality about it, says Robert Menzies.[27] It is not merely an interesting discussion, or a brilliant discourse, or a thoughtful interpretation, or an emotional lamentation. An evangelistic sermon may be any of those, but it must also be an appeal for a decision, for a change of mind and heart, for a new resolve, a new commitment, a new priority. The sense of urgency and the importance of the appeal must be communicated by the preacher's style. Some preachers need to be reminded that increasing the volume is not the only way to communicate urgency. Some have laughed at but have not learned from the preacher who wrote in the margin of his sermon manuscript, "Argument weak here. Shout louder!"

Sometimes a whisper is far more compelling than a shout. Whatever your style, the hearers must perceive that you not only believe the message but that you are desperately anxious for them to believe it as well. The appeal is often given added urgency in evangelistic preaching by an invitation to respond in some symbolic or tangible way—coming forward or standing in place, signing a card or raising a hand, speaking to a counselor or meeting with some elders, being baptized or attending a class. At other times it is a matter of inviting personal prayer and reflection about whatever the appeal may have been. Regardless of whether or not there is some tangible action at the time, there is never any mistaking the need to respond and the urgency of the appeal. It is senseless, however, to ask for a decision at the end of the sermon unless there has been adequate preparation for it throughout the sermon. The appeal should never be perceived to be an afterthought.

Patience. The urgency of the preacher is balanced by the patience of the pastor, whose concern is for the end result and whose evangelism reflects a sensitivity to proper pace and timing. One can distinguish here between the evangelical whose language becomes a barrier to decision and the evangelist whose language is geared to the level of the hearer's understanding. The decision called for must be one the hearer understands and can make with integrity. The appeal to make that decision, to take that next step of faith, is no less urgent because it is not expressed in the vernacular of fundamentalism. Those who pride themselves on being evangelical are often more concerned with the language that is used than with the evangelistic result. If they have used the proper language, they feel they have fulfilled all righteousness. It's not their fault if the other person does not respond. Pastor-evangelists, on the other hand, are concerned about persons. Their pastoral concern sensitizes their evangelistic style, and their evangelistic concern informs their pastoral approach. Both as pastor and as evangelist they are willing to trust the Holy Spirit, believing that God's timing is always best.

The Preacher's Sense of Direction

Related to style and content as well as to the planning process is the preacher's sense of direction. There must be movement to the entire preaching ministry as well as to an individual sermon, and each sermon has to fit into the overall plan. Where are you going—in what direction are you trying to lead your people? That is not as easy a question to answer as it appears. For one thing, you know that your congregation is always changing. Even in the most stable church, you are not preaching to the same people every Sunday. Not only do the faces change, but the circumstances and needs of the people behind the faces are constantly changing. So is the world about them constantly changing, and what happens in some faraway place can have a sudden drastic impact on the folks in Middletown, U.S.A. A plane is hijacked, a volcano erupts, a tornado strikes, and some people's lives are unexpectedly changed.

Thus you are preaching to a different congregation every Sunday. How then can you hope to lead them in any direction? How can you move them from one point to another as a congregation in their pilgrimage of faith, when some of the people you are preaching to this week were not there last week, and some were not there the week before? How do you move people from a point some of them haven't reached yet? On any given Sunday, some of the people will not have heard what you said last week, let alone last year. Even if they were there, did they actually hear it? And even if they heard it, do they remember it? And even if they remember it, do they understand it? And even if they understand it, do they still believe it? And what about the people who are there for the first time? They have never heard you preach at all! And what if they have never been to *any* church before?

In view of such diversity, how can anyone talk about direction and movement in preaching? The only answer I know to the dilemma is to strive for a balance that takes seriously this diversity. Each sermon, on the one hand, has to have its own message, independent of what was said in any previous sermon, for the benefit of the people who are there for the first time. On the other hand, each sermon has to build on what has been said before, for the benefit of the people who have been attending regularly. It is with the latter group that there has to be some direction in preaching, but the movement is not at a steady rate. Every now and then you have to go back and pick up the people who were not there when you dealt with the theme before, but you do it in a way that will still have fresh meaning for those who were there. If you're doing a series, you recap what has already been covered, so that visitors and newcomers alike will feel they are up to date. A diagram of the movement would look like this:

Another evangelistic benefit of this style is that people may feel regretful that they missed what went before, and, better yet, decide they want to be there for the next installment. People need to learn that when they aren't in church, they may miss the very sermon they needed most to hear. And church hoppers need to understand that for the same reason they will have a much clearer picture and better understanding of the whole gospel if they listen regularly to the same preacher than they will if they bounce around from church to church. People who attend their own church irregularly and people who hop from one church to another every Sunday will not experience the benefits of a preaching ministry with direction, one that is designed to lead them forward in their faith walk.

Having direction means, furthermore, stretching but not snapping people's thinking strings. The pastor-evangelist preaches at a level that will demand people's close attention and careful thought but not confound them or confuse them. It is not always possible to wrap everything up neatly at the end of a sermon. It is often better to leave things to the imagination of the hearers and let them draw their own conclusion or make their own application. Sometimes it is more effective to be suggestive rather than definitive. What you say may sound better in the indicative than in the imperative mood. Again, that calls for a sensitive awareness on the preacher's part of where people are. The pastor-evangelist reads their faces and body language very carefully from the pulpit. It's not a matter of delivering a speech but of preaching to people. It's not a performance. If you preach *to* people rather than *for* them, you can tell when you are not getting through.

The Preacher's Method

Much of what we have been discussing in the preceding pages has to do with method. But if you ask most ministers, "What is your method of preaching?" chances are they will say something like "I preach from notes" or "I memorize my sermons" or "I use a manuscript." Then they will go on to describe in more detail where they get their ideas, how they file their illustrations, how they use the Bible, whether they are topical or expository preachers, when and how they write their sermons, whether they use a typewriter, a computer, or a tape recorder, how long they spend on the process, what they hope to accomplish in their preaching ministry, how they file their sermons, and so on.[28]

At this point I am using the word "method" in the initial and narrow sense to refer only to the preacher's use of a manuscript, notes, or whatever. I have already stated my conviction that you should choose the method of delivery with which you are most comfortable and which enables you to communicate most effectively with your hearers. Usually the more direct eye contact you have with your congregation, the better. If you use a manuscript, don't read it to them, *speak* it to them. You can't appeal for a response with your head buried in your manuscript. If you have memorized your sermon, don't read it off the back of your mind; speak it from the bottom of your heart.

Whatever the method, the pastor-evangelist takes seriously God's role in the preaching event. No sermon should ever appear to be so studied and practiced that there is no room for the Holy Spirit to operate on the preacher as well as on the congregation. It is not our method but God's grace that saves people. A method is a means to an end, not an end in itself. So we choose the method that best frees us to be open and useful to the Holy Spirit.

There is one more point to be made: having a method with which we are most comfortable does not mean we should be limited to only one method. The content of the sermon often determines which method is best. A first-person sermon may have to be memorized, for example. Some sermons can be preached more easily from notes than others. We do not have to make those decisions entirely on our own, for the Holy Spirit, who helps us choose our topic, will also help us choose the method, if, as we have said again and again, we undergird the whole enterprise with prayer.

In examining the task of preaching from an evangelistic perspective, we have by no means exhausted the subject of preaching, but I hope we have been able sufficiently for our purposes to identify the characteristics of evangelistic preaching or, to put it more precisely, what it means to preach with evangelistic sensitivity. We have not yet discussed at any length the content of the message itself, and to that important subject we turn in the next chapter.

10

Presenting
the Gospel

Most preachers would define an evangelistic sermon primarily in terms of the basic thrust or aim, which is to present the gospel in order that people may respond. That is what distinguishes the word "evangelistic" from the word "evangelical." A sermon can be evangelical without being evangelistic, but it cannot be evangelistic without being evangelical. Simply defined, evangelical means gospel-related. Obviously an evangelistic sermon has to be gospel-related, but its aim is for people to respond in faith, to make a commitment of faith. A preacher could use evangelical language without asking for a decision. The moment an appeal is made, an evangelical sermon becomes evangelistic.

Sometimes evangelical language can actually be a barrier to evangelism. If we drown prospective church members in too much of the blood of the Lamb, they may tune us out or turn us off. We have to use evangelical terms with evangelistic sensitivity. Given that sensitivity, the content of an evangelistic sermon should be gospel-oriented, with a strong emphasis on personal commitment to Jesus Christ. Evangelistic preaching takes seriously the reality of human sin and stresses the need for repentance and conversion. The person and work of Christ, his death and resurrection, the forgiveness of sins, and the promise of eternal life are standard themes of an evangelistic sermon, always delivered, as pointed out in the last chapter, with an urgent appeal for decision.

The central theme of Jesus' preaching was the kingdom of God, which refers both to the realm and to the reign of God.

The parables that Jesus used in his teachings about the kingdom reveal its paradoxical nature. The kingdom is something only God can bring about, and yet we are to seek it. It is present and yet to come, fulfilled in Christ but not yet consummated. The kingdom is God's, not ours: God's to build and God's to give. The signs of the kingdom are the words and works of Jesus, whom to accept or to reject is to accept or reject the kingdom.

Matthew's Gospel in all but three instances uses the expression "the kingdom of heaven," whereas Mark and Luke speak only of "the kingdom of God." The two expressions mean the same thing: "God ruling" or "God reigning." John's Gospel has only two references to the kingdom of God. Paul and Peter also refer to the kingdom of Christ (Eph. 5:5; 2 Peter 1:11). "If the message of evangelism has an appropriate kingdom emphasis, it will be Trinitarian in its expression and church-related in its orientation. The fact that the kingdom is the rule of God is the basis and thrust of the social gospel. . . . The message of evangelism, therefore, must include the good news of the kingdom, in the manner of him whom to know as Savior and to serve as Lord is the way to the kingdom, the truth of the kingdom, and the life in the kingdom."[29]

There are as many definitions of evangelism as there are people writing on the subject. Purely and simply, evangelism is the proclamation of the gospel, or the sharing of the good news of Jesus Christ. Most definitions are more descriptive than definitive, but they are important in that they indicate what the definers have in mind when they use the term. In the light of the kingdom emphasis described above, I have suggested the following expanded definition of evangelism:

> Evangelism is
> > proclaiming in word and deed
> > the good news of the kingdom of God
> > and
> > calling people to repentance,
> > to personal faith in Jesus Christ as Lord and Savior,

to active membership in the church,
and to obedient service in the world.[30]

If evangelistic preaching is not thought of in terms of a particular type of sermon that is delivered on Evangelism Sunday or Decision Day or some other special day, then we have to ask, What should the content of *any* sermon be in order for it to be called evangelistic? Given the need for personal decision and the urgency of the appeal, we could say that unless the message contains some aspect of the gospel, it is not an evangelistic sermon. Some preachers would say it should not even be called a sermon.

Once again, the distinction may be mostly a matter of degree, but it is plain that evangelistic preaching, by definition, has to be clearly related to the gospel. The word "clearly" is significant, for the sermon can be related to the gospel without the use of evangelical language. I have preached sermons from the Old Testament in which there was much reference to God and an urgent call for a decision of faith, but no direct reference to the gospel. Was I not being evangelistic that Sunday? The answer to that question lies elsewhere than in the sermon.

The Where of the Gospel

Consider the context in which the preaching takes place. A particular sermon may not have been evangelical or evangelistic in the strict sense, but the worship service always was! The sermon was always in the context of a worship service, and somewhere in the service the gospel was clearly presented, perhaps in the prayer immediately following the sermon, or in the pastoral prayer, or in remarks made just before the benediction, or when introducing a hymn, or during the announcements, or at some other appropriate place in the service. Usually the relationship between the Old Testament theme and the Christian gospel was made clear in the sermon itself, but sometimes it was effective to make the gospel reference and appeal somewhere else. It is extremely important for the pastor-evangelist to remember that preaching is in the context of worship, and the whole service is the medium for evangelism.

Nor does there have to be an altar call following every sermon in order for the service to have an evangelistic thrust. The message on a given Sunday may not lend itself to such an appeal, in which case the worship leader might give some sort of invitation elsewhere in the service. For example, you could incorporate an invitation in your welcome to visitors. Or, after the corporate prayer of confession and the assurance of pardon, you might invite anyone who would like to talk privately about what it means to confess one's sins and to accept God's forgiveness to meet with you after the service. Or at the time of the Apostles' Creed you might say, "This is an affirmation of what we believe. If you are wrestling with any aspect of the Creed and would like to discuss it with one of our faith counselors, you are invited to meet in the church parlor after the service." Or again, at the time of the offering, you might say something like this: "As you give your offering this morning, think about what it means to give your whole life to Jesus Christ. If any of you would like to commit your life to Christ for the first time, or recommit your life to him, why don't you indicate it on one of the pew cards and place it in the plate with your offering. And if you would like to talk about it, I'll be in my study from two o'clock to four o'clock this afternoon." Or again, "If you really meant the words of the hymn we just sang and if you understand their relevance for your life, I hope you will mention it to me as you leave church this morning."

Having seen the need to view the sermon in the context of the total worship experience, we still have to evaluate a sermon on its own merits in terms of evangelistic thrust. If, as we have said, an evangelistic sermon must be clearly gospel-related with an appeal for a decision, what are the various aspects of the gospel to look for in a sermon?

The What of the Gospel

Following the pattern set by the heading of the previous section, this refers to the historical facts and events of Jesus' life. The gospel story has its own self-authenticating evangelistic impact. Those who have served on the mission fields know how impressed godly people of other faiths can be by the words and works, the life and death of Jesus. What Christian parents have not discovered how much their children love to hear the story of Jesus?

Believers also respond to the story, as Katherine Hankey's gospel song reminds us:

> I love to tell the story;
>   For those who know it best
> Seem hungering and thirsting
>   To hear it, like the rest.

Many years ago I heard a dramatic preacher tell the passion story so vividly that I felt as if I were actually there, and for the first time in my life I felt something of the agony of the cross and understood in a new way what God in Christ had done for *me*. The preacher drew no lessons from the story; he simply told it. But what a powerful impression it made on me and, judging from their rapt attention, on most everyone else in the chapel that night. The story, properly told, is amazingly effective. It is an unending source of the best illustrations of all. Evangelistic preaching is compatible with narrative theology, for the pastor-evangelist knows the value of helping people to see that they have a faith story and to understand how their story relates to *the* story.[31]

The Why of the Gospel

There are valid reasons for believing the Why of the gospel. They have to do with the evidence provided by the gospel witnesses. Their testimony is the reason why you and I can believe the story is true.

The eyewitnesses. The lives and testimonies of the persons who knew Jesus are another aspect of the gospel that can have an evangelistic effect. One Easter, I preached a sermon on the Sadducees entitled "They Said It Couldn't Be Done." It sometimes surprises modern skeptics to hear about this opposition party who did not believe in the resurrection of the dead. I have always presented the resurrection as an affirmation of faith, which cannot be proved. In this particular sermon, however, I decided to present the scriptural evidence for the resurrection as if I were a lawyer presenting a case. The following excerpt is from my summary statement to the "jury" (the congregation):

> Faith does not mean the blind acceptance of an idea. Faith means the willingness to accept evidence. Faith is our belief in the testimony of the apostles. They have presented us with certain evidence. The question is, Do we accept it? Are they reliable witnesses?
>
> They are indeed reliable! There are many reasons why. Let me mention just one. The persons who wrote the New Testament testify of themselves that they were slow to accept the fact of the resurrection. They would not believe the women who discovered the empty tomb. They did not recognize their Lord at first. They had to touch him, to make sure he was real. . . . They wanted proof. Far from thinking of perpetrating a fraud, far from being susceptible to the hallucinations of wishful thinking, the disciples were discouraged and depressed, lacking in understanding, unimaginative. Even when they saw the empty tomb, John and Peter still could not put two and two together, "for as yet they did not know the scripture, that he must rise from the dead."
>
> These were the witnesses of the risen Jesus. Their *doubt* is one of the best reasons for our *faith!* Because they had to be convinced *then,* you and I can be convinced *now.* Believing in the resurrection is not like believing in Santa Claus. The Easter story is not a fairy tale. It is, to the heart of faith, a historical fact—utterly amazing, incredibly stupendous, totally inexplicable, but a fact of faith, nevertheless.

What people say about your sermon tells you more about them than it does about your sermon. What you hope is that different people will be responding in different ways every Sunday, so you will know you are reaching a wide spectrum. If the same few people are the only ones commenting, you may be on too narrow a track. Be that as it may, I was completely surprised by the reactions that Easter. There were many lawyers in the congregation, and whereas I had wondered if they might be skeptical about the "evidence" I presented, they were most enthusiastic. "I never realized that our belief is grounded in that kind of evidence," said one man. "I've always thought I had to take the resurrection on blind faith."

That is only one of many examples I could cite of the evangelistic impact of the testimony of eyewitnesses to the Jesus story. The apostle Paul is more to us than a brilliant thinker, theologian, and missionary. He was also a witness to the resurrected Christ: "Last of all, as to one untimely born, he appeared also to me" (1 Cor. 15:8). That for Paul was a justification for his authority. "Am I not an apostle?" he asked the Corinthians. "Have I not seen Jesus our Lord?" (1 Cor. 9:1). His belief is a reason for me to believe *what* I believe is true. So is the faith of Peter, James, John, and all the other disciples.

The scriptures. Another reason is the witness of the scriptures, especially the Gospels, which are faith portraits rather than historical biographies. Each of the writers paints a picture of Jesus as he saw him, emphasizing what for each were the important features of the portrait. Critics delight in pointing out the discrepancies in the reports, but the discrepancies themselves lend credence to the accounts. Although there are minor variations, there is also an astonishing consistency among them, resulting in a composite picture of our Lord that is beautifully and convincingly integrated.

It has been often said that the Bible has been subjected to more intensive critical analysis and scientific scrutiny than any other book ever written. All that analysis has increased rather than diminished its incomparable value and authority.

It is God's decisive word to us today, as it has been to Christians in all ages. The written word bears witness to the living Word, who "became flesh and dwelt among us, full of grace and truth" (John 1:14).

The Gospel writers took great pains to show that Jesus was the Messiah of whom the prophets had written and for whose coming Israel had long been waiting and hoping. So we find Matthew saying again and again, "This was to fulfil what was spoken by the prophet." And Jesus himself declared that he was the one to whom the scriptures bore witness. After reading a passage from the prophet Isaiah, he astounded the people of his hometown when he declared in the synagogue at Nazareth, "Today this scripture has been fulfilled in your hearing" (Luke 4:21). On another occasion, in Jerusalem, when he was being criticized for healing a man on the Sabbath, Jesus replied, "You search the scriptures, because you think that in them you have eternal life; and it is they that bear witness to me" (John 5:39).

Jesus shocked the religious authorities by reinterpreting the scriptures. "You have heard that it was said . . . but I say to you" (Matt. 5:21–22, 27–28, 31–32, 33–34, 38–39, 43–44). He challenged those who were bound to the letter to live by the spirit of the law. "Think not that I have come to abolish the law and the prophets," he said in the Sermon on the Mount: "I have come not to abolish them but to fulfil them" (Matt. 5:17). Jesus knew his destiny. "Let the scriptures be fulfilled," he said, as he was being arrested in the Garden of Gethsemane.

For those who view it through the eyes of a Christ-centered faith, the Old Testament is a convincing reason for believing that Jesus was who he said he was, the fulfillment of the law and the prophets. The Jews still await their Messiah, but Christians proclaim that the Messiah has already come. With Peter we have believed, and have come to know, that he is the Holy One of God. He is the Christ!

The Holy Spirit. The ultimate witness to the truth of the gospel is the Holy Spirit, who authenticates all other witnesses and without whose testimony no one could believe.

"When the Counselor comes," Jesus told his disciples, "whom I shall send to you from the Father, even the Spirit of truth, who proceeds from the Father, he will bear witness to me" (John 15:26). Peter and the disciples told the Sanhedrin, "We are witnesses to these things, and so is the Holy Spirit whom God has given to those who obey him" (Acts 5:32). Despite the biblical evidence, we know we cannot prove the resurrection to ourselves or to anyone else. It is a fact of faith, not a logical necessity. The reason I believe in the resurrection is that I have come to know the living Christ. Harry Webb Farrington's hymn says it well:

> I know not how that Bethlehem's Babe
>   Could in the Godhead be;
> I only know the Manger child
>   Has brought God's life to me.
>
> I know not how that Calvary's cross
>   A world from sin could free;
> I only know its matchless love
>   Has brought God's love to me.
>
> I know not how that Joseph's tomb
>   Could solve death's mystery;
> I only know a living Christ,
>   Our immortality.

A sermon that helps people to understand the role of the Holy Spirit in their decision of faith is presenting a crucial aspect of the gospel.

The Who of the Gospel

The good news, in a word, is Jesus. He is the Who of the gospel, the subject and the object of our faith, the absolutely unique fact of the Christian proclamation. "We preach Christ crucified," said Paul (1 Cor. 1:23).

The proclamational heart of the gospel is that Jesus is Lord and Savior. This is the basic affirmation of faith that defines the confessional relationship of every Christian to Jesus

Christ. We proclaim him to be the Savior of the world and
our personal savior, the Lord of the universe and Lord of our
lives. "We have seen and testify," wrote John, "that the
Father has sent his Son as the Savior of the world" (1 John
4:14). Peter's second letter concludes with the exhortation to
"grow in the grace and knowledge of our Lord and Savior
Jesus Christ. To him be the glory both now and to the day
of eternity. Amen" (2 Peter 3:18).

Evangelistic preaching attempts to help all people understand the meaning and to take seriously the implications of
that affirmation, and it confronts them with the necessity of
a decision of faith. "Who was this person and who is he to
me, this Jesus who made such fantastic claims about himself? Was he or was he not what he said he was?" To accept
him as Lord and Savior is to accept the claims of Christ, who
said:

I am the way, and the truth, and the life; no one comes to
the Father, but by me. (John 14:6)

Whoever has seen me has seen the Father. . . . Do you not
believe that I am in the Father and the Father in me? (John
14:9–10)

I and the Father are one. (John 10:30)

But I am among you as one who serves. (Luke 22:27)

I am the bread of life; whoever comes to me shall not
hunger, and whoever believes in me shall never thirst. (John
6:35)

I am the living bread which came down from heaven; if any
one eats of this bread, that person will live for ever. (John
6:51)

I am the light of the world; whoever follows me will not
walk in darkness, but will have the light of life. (John 8:12)

I am the door of the sheep. . . . I came that they may have
life, and have it abundantly. (John 10:7, 10)

I am the resurrection and the life. . . . Whoever lives and believes in me shall never die. (John 11:25–26)

I am the vine, you are the branches. . . . Apart from me you can do nothing. (John 15:5)

And lo, I am with you always, to the close of the age. (Matt. 28:20)

The presentation of the gospel must sooner or later confront people with the "I ams" of Jesus. And the question that remains for every person who hears them is the question that Jesus addressed to his disciples: "But who do you say that I am?" (Luke 9:20).

Sincere seekers, reverent agnostics, and persons who are wrestling with or who have made the decision to join the church need to hear this aspect of the gospel. In their consuming passion for growth, some churches, I fear, have made it too easy for people to join. There is little if any preparation for membership, and their reception is only a formality, in which the meaning of the membership vows is lost. The perfunctory nature of the process robs what should be an inspirational event of its integrity. The brief message that you preach at the service of reception, if there is one, can reinforce the preparation for membership and focus the attention of all present on the central affirmation of the gospel, that Jesus Christ is Lord and Savior.

Those joining the church are not the only persons who need to be challenged to think about the Lordship and Saviorhood of Jesus Christ. Nominal members and those persons who at the time they made their profession of faith never really came to grips with what it means to accept Christ as Lord and Savior need to be challenged continually from the pulpit to do so, not in a way that implies a lack of sincerity on their part, not judgmentally or accusingly, but in a way that inspires them to take a new look at their commitment. They need constantly to be thinking about what it means to be Christ's person in the world today.

The How of the Gospel

Someone might wonder why the affirmation of Jesus' Lordship and Saviorhood is good news. One obvious reason is that if Jesus is Lord of the universe and the Savior of the world, he can, as the saying goes, deliver on his promises. "For all the promises of God find their Yes in him," declared Paul (2 Cor. 1:20). The promises of the gospel are the answer to the How question: How do we deal with the three basic problems that beset all humanity?

The problem of sin. How can a God of justice and righteousness accept the likes of us? The gospel acknowledges the universality of human sin. "None is righteous," confessed Paul, quoting the psalmist, "no, not one. . . . All have sinned and fall short of the glory of God" (Rom. 3:10, 23). That is a reality known to all who honestly examine themselves in the light of God's truth. John put it squarely: "If we say we have no sin, we deceive ourselves, and the truth is not in us" (1 John 1:8).

The answer to the problem of sin is the gospel's promise of forgiveness. So we hear Peter proclaiming to the household of Cornelius regarding Jesus, "To him all the prophets bear witness that every one who believes in him receives forgiveness of sins through his name" (Acts 10:43). "Let it be known to you therefore, brethren," declared Paul to the gathering in the synagogue at Antioch of Pisidia, "that through this man forgiveness of sins is proclaimed to you, and by him every one that believes is freed from everything from which you could not be freed by the law of Moses" (Acts 13:38–39).

For all lost souls struggling to prove themselves acceptable to God yet knowing the truth of Paul's words that no human being can be justified in God's sight by good works (Rom. 3:20), the promise of forgiveness is good news indeed. Those who are encumbered by their own guilt, those who have given up the hope of a new beginning, those whose confidence rests in their own righteousness, all need to hear the promise of the forgiveness which is made known and available to us through Jesus Christ. It is an evangelistic note that should be sounded often in our preaching.

The problem of death. In addition to sin, there is also the problem of our mortality. The beauty of these oft-quoted lines from Thomas Gray's "Elegy Written in a Country Churchyard" does not disguise the somber reality of their message:

> The boast of heraldry, the pomp of power,
>   And all that beauty, all that wealth e'er gave,
> Awaits alike th' inevitable hour:
>   The paths of glory lead but to the grave.

Is the writer of Ecclesiastes correct, then, in his gloomy assessment that all is vanity? People may jokingly say "You can't take it with you," but sooner or later the reality of their finitude strikes home, and at that point the gospel promise of eternal life can burst through their morbid gloom like a sunray piercing the black clouds of a summer thunderstorm. "For God so loved the world that he gave his only Son, that whoever believes in him should not perish but have eternal life. . . . Whoever believes in the Son has eternal life" (John 3:16, 36).

And what is eternal life? One definition is given us in Jesus' great intercessory prayer, which John has recorded in his own unique style: "And this is eternal life, that they know thee the only true God, and Jesus Christ whom thou hast sent" (John 17:3). It is a present possibility, a point plainly made by John in his first letter: "I write this to you who believe in the name of the Son of God, that you may know that you have eternal life" (1 John 5:13). "That you *have* eternal life"—present tense!

Among the persons attending a Lenten Bible study that I was conducting one evening was the middle-aged son of a learned New Testament theologian. In the sharing time at the end of the evening, this man who had grown up in a Christian home and who was himself an elder in his church commented that he had never realized that eternal life begins now. "What an exciting discovery!" he exclaimed to the group. "I always thought it was something that happened when you die!''

It is easy for us preachers to assume that everyone knows and understands the gospel, but that is not the case. We have to remind people continually of the gospel promise of eternal life, which, if it is understood, will surely be heard as good news. Only then can they resonate with the confidence of Paul, when he wrote to the Roman Christians, ''I am sure that neither death, nor life, nor angels, nor principalities, nor things present, nor things to come, nor powers, nor height, nor depth, nor anything else in all creation, will be able to separate us from the love of God in Christ Jesus our Lord'' (Rom. 8:38–39).

The hope of eternal life is grounded in our faith in the resurrection of Jesus Christ, whose death on the cross, though a noble sacrifice, would have been only a horrible tragedy and history's cruelest irony, if the story had ended on Calvary. There is no denying the truth of Paul's assertion to the church at Corinth: ''If Christ has not been raised, then our preaching is in vain and your faith is in vain. We are even found to be misrepresenting God, because we testified of God that he raised Christ. . . . If Christ has not been raised, your faith is futile and you are still in your sins. Then those also who have fallen asleep in Christ have perished'' (1 Cor. 15:14–18). Any gospel that ignores, omits, or mitigates the resurrection, therefore, is a truncated gospel. If we fail to proclaim the good news of the promise of eternal life, we fail to offer people the Christian answer to the problem of death.

The problem of coping. Jesus came to show us not how to die, but how to live. ''I came that they may have life,'' he said, ''and have it abundantly'' (John 10:10). But what is the abundant life, and how do we live it in the world such as ours? The gospel is simple, but our lives are complex and the problems of confronting the world today are overwhelming. We have transplanted organs, communicated with chimpanzees, and set foot on the moon, but we haven't learned to live together in peace. As individuals we face the daily pressures of our obligations at home and at work, the demands imposed upon us by our employers, our families, our neighbors, our friends, the government, society in general, and the world about us. We are frustrated because we can't control our own destiny. We struggle to keep our heads above water, paying our bills, holding on to our jobs, caring for our families, worrying about their health and safety, maintaining our homes, keeping up with our friends, educating our children, providing for the future, dealing with accidents and calamities, disappointments and defeats, temptations and mistakes, sickness and suffering, sorrow and bereavement. The desperate plea from the pews is not just how to handle the problem of death but how to cope with the problems of life!

The answer to the problem of coping is Jesus' promise to be with us always, fulfilled in the gift of the Holy Spirit. So Paul could say to the Romans, "We rejoice in our sufferings, knowing that suffering produces endurance, and endurance produces character, and character produces hope, and hope does not disappoint us, because God's love has been poured into our hearts through the Holy Spirit which has been given to us" (Rom. 5:3–5). Paul is a good role model for us, because he knew the secret of Christian contentment. "I have learned, in whatever state I am, to be content," he told the Philippians. "I know how to be abased, and I know how to abound; in any and all circumstances I have learned the secret of facing plenty and hunger, abundance and want. I can do all things in him who strengthens me" (Phil. 4:11–13).

Paul's life is a testimony to the fact that being a Christian is no escape hatch from the problems of life. On the contrary, his sufferings began after he became a Christian. God does not spare us the consequences of our own mistakes and the natural shocks that flesh is heir to, but God gives us the strength to endure and the faith to know that "in everything God works for good with those who love him" (Rom. 8:28). Paul knew that nothing can separate us from the love of God (Rom. 8:39). "God is faithful," he told the Corinthians, "and he will not let you be tempted beyond your strength, but with the temptation will also provide the way of escape, that you may be able to endure it" (1 Cor. 10:13). Paul could endure his "thorn in the flesh," because he knew that God's grace is sufficient and God's power is made perfect in human weakness. "I will all the more gladly boast of my weaknesses," he told the Corinthians, "that the power of Christ may rest upon me. For the sake of Christ, then, I am content with weaknesses, insults, hardships, persecutions, and calamities; for when I am weak, then I am strong" (2 Cor. 12:9–10).

Peter picks up the same theme, reminding us that the genuineness of our faith is tested by suffering (1 Peter 1:6–7), and the writer of the letter to the Hebrews points us to Jesus, "who endured from sinners such hostility against himself, so that you may not grow weary or fainthearted" (Heb. 12:3). The writer also knew the secret of contentment, exhorting his hearers to keep their lives "free from love of money, and be content with what you have; for he has said, 'I will never fail you nor forsake you.' Hence we can confidently say, 'The Lord is my helper, I will not be afraid' " (Heb. 13:5–6).

Yes, there are problems, and everyone has them. But the good news is that God can help us to cope, whatever the problem may be. God guides and God provides, when we are in tune with the Holy Spirit. In our preaching we need not avoid, nor dare we deny, the realities of life. Indeed, much if not most of our preaching will be devoted to the problems of human existence, but the pastor-evangelist will always remind people of God's steadfast love and Jesus' promise to be with us to the end of the age. The application of that truth to difficult personal problems and complex social issues may well be the aspect of the gospel which most frequently needs to be heard. It may be in search of the answer to the problem of coping that more people are drawn to the church than for any other reason. It can have, therefore, a powerful evangelistic impact.

The If of the Gospel

One question we need to address at this point is whether the promises of the gospel are offered conditionally or unconditionally. Is there an "if" clause attached? We preach about unconditional grace, declaring that God loves us with no strings attached. Yet there appear to be certain provisos for receiving the gift of salvation. Consider the following examples:

Whoever endures to the end will be saved. (Matt. 10:22; cf. 24:13; Mark 13:13)

Truly, I say to you, unless you turn and become like children, you will never enter the kingdom of heaven. (Matt. 18:3; cf. Mark 10:15; Luke 18:17)

Whoever believes and is baptized will be saved; but whoever does not believe will be condemned. (Mark 16:16)

And behold, a lawyer stood up to put him to the test, saying, "Teacher, what shall I do to inherit eternal life?" He said to him, "What is written in the law? How do you read?" And he answered, "You shall love the Lord your God with all your heart, and with all your soul, and with all your strength, and with all your mind; and your neighbor as yourself." And he said to him, "You have answered right; do this, and you will live." (Luke 10:25–28)

Truly, truly, I say to you, unless one is born anew, one cannot see the kingdom of God. (John 3:3)

If you love me, you will keep my commandments. . . . Whoever has my commandments and keeps them, that is the person who loves me; and whoever loves me will be loved by my Father. (John 14:15, 21)

If you keep my commandments, you will abide in my love, just as I have kept my Father's commandments and abide in his love. (John 15:10)

And Peter said to them, "Repent, and be baptized every one of you in the name of Jesus Christ for the forgiveness of your sins; and you shall receive the gift of the Holy Spirit." (Acts 2:38)

Repent therefore, and turn again, that your sins may be blotted out. (Acts 3:19)

The Pastor-Evangelist as Preacher

[The jailer] brought them out and said, "Men, what must I do to be saved?" And they said, "Believe in the Lord Jesus, and you will be saved, you and your household." (Acts 16:30–31)

All who have sinned without the law will also perish without the law, and all who have sinned under the law will be judged by the law. For it is not the hearers of the law who are righteous before God, but the doers of the law who will be justified. (Rom. 2:12–13)

If you confess with your lips that Jesus is Lord and believe in your heart that God raised him from the dead, you will be saved. . . . For, "every one who calls upon the name of the Lord will be saved." (Rom. 10:9, 13)

Do you not know that the unrighteous will not inherit the kingdom of God? (1 Cor. 6:9)

Yet [we] know that a person is not justified by works of the law but through faith in Jesus Christ. (Gal. 2:16)

You see that a person is justified by works and not by faith alone. (James 2:24)

And this is his commandment, that we should believe in the name of his Son Jesus Christ and love one another, just as he has commanded us. All who keep his commandments abide in him, and he in them. (1 John 3:23–24)

These are but a few of the references that could be cited to justify the conclusion that the gospel promises are conditional. How do we reconcile their conditional nature with our belief in the unconditional nature of God's love? It is another unresolvable paradox, which can be only stated, not explained. We can say that God's love is unconditionally offered but conditionally received. The gospel promises are universal but contingent.

Another way of understanding the conditional-unconditional paradox is to consider the three-dimensional nature of salvation, expressed in the familiar apothegm, "I have been saved, I am being saved, I hope to be saved." We have been saved (a past event) by the redemptive act of God in the death, resurrection, and ascension of Jesus. We are being saved (a present process) by the sanctifying work of the Holy Spirit, who calls, transforms, nurtures, equips, and renews us daily in service to the Lord Jesus Christ. We hope to be saved (a future possibility) in the eschaton, whenever that comes.

The assurance of salvation is an affirmation of faith in the reality of the resurrection event. The evidence of salvation is the present experience of God's love and grace in the lives of those who believe in and follow Jesus Christ as Lord and Savior. The hope of salvation is trusting acceptance of Jesus' promise of the gift of eternal life to all who believe in him. The first dimension is unconditional; Christ died for the whole world. The third dimension is contingent upon the second. How we live determines whether we receive the promises. From the foregoing list of scripture references we see that our receiving the promise is contingent upon our belief in Jesus Christ, including repentance, conversion, baptism, spiritual rebirth, patient endurance, worthy deeds, keeping the commandments, and a public profession of faith.

Inasmuch as it is often directed to the unchurched, evangelistic preaching is characterized by its strong emphasis on the necessity of repentance and conversion. The New Testament word for repentance is *metanoia,* which conveys the idea of a change of mind and heart. It expresses the rich meaning of the Hebrew word *shub,* which occurs more than a thousand times in the Old Testament, almost always conveying the idea of "returning" or "going back again." Since the prophets viewed sin as turning away from God, so *shub* was understood as turning back to God again with one's whole being. It involved obedience to God's will, unconditional trust in God, and the renunciation of everything ungodly.[32] Repentance, therefore, is not just saying you're sorry, or feeling sorry. It is determining to make amends and doing something about it. Repentance is essential to being converted, the Greek word for which is *epistrephō*: literally,

"turn." It involves a complete turnaround, a new orientation, a new focus, a totally new commitment.

Those who are looking for cheap grace need to hear the
conditions of the gospel. Salvation may be free, but it is not
automatic. We were bought for a price by one "who, though
he was in the form of God, did not count equality with God
a thing to be grasped, but emptied himself, taking the form
of a servant. . . . And being found in human form he
humbled himself and became obedient unto death, even
death on a cross" (Phil. 2:6–8). It is he who bids us deny
ourselves and take up our cross and follow him (Matt. 16:24;
Mark 8:34; Luke 9:23).

The gospel conditions are the answer to those who are
wondering, What must I do to be saved? To be sure, the God
we believe in is able to save whomever he will, whenever,
wherever, and however he will, despite our faults and
failures. God's love can transcend any or all conditions.
"For God sent the Son into the world, not to condemn the
world, but that the world might be saved through him" (John
3:17). Though the world deserves it, Jesus came not to
condemn the world but to save it. We need to help people
understand what it means to be saved, lest the expression be
what it has become for some, a pious cliché.

Maybe there are people in the pews who are wondering,
when they hear those words, From what are we saved?
We're saved from the fear of death, not from dying but from
the horrible emptiness and finality of the grave, so that Paul
could exclaim, "O death, where is thy victory? O death,
where is thy sting?" (1 Cor. 15:55). We're saved from the
fear of death, because death cannot separate us from the love
of God. We're saved from the burden of our guilt and shame,
because God has forgiven us in Christ. We're saved from
having to justify ourselves by our own good works, because
no one can. We're saved from having to prove ourselves
acceptable to God, because in Christ we have learned that
God accepts us the way we are.

That is what we are saved *from*, but what are we saved *for*?
We have to help people see salvation's obligations as well as

its benefits. Our salvation is for a purpose. We're saved for fellowship and service. We're saved in order that we may have fellowship with God and with each other (1 John 1:3–4). We're saved that we may glorify God and enjoy God forever. We're saved to serve God by serving others. We're saved that we may have the peace that passes understanding, the joy that knows no bounds, the hope that never disappoints us. We're saved that we may have the strength, the power, the confidence, the sense of purpose that only God can give. All this is ours for the asking, because God so loved the world. All this is ours, *if* . . . !

The Therefores of the Gospel

Therefores refer to the demands of the gospel. Whereas the conditions of the gospel are directed especially to the unchurched, the demands of the gospel apply to those who have already accepted it. The conditions for receiving the gospel promises become the demands upon those who have received them.

The Great Commandment. "If you love me," said Jesus, "you will keep my commandments" (John 14:15). "This is my commandment, that you love one another as I have loved you" (John 15:12). In his reply to the man who asked him what was the greatest commandment, Jesus indicated the nature and extent of the love he demands of his followers: You shall love the Lord your God with all your heart, soul, mind, and strength, and your neighbor as yourself (Mark 12:30–31). In the light of that commandment, we know how far short we fall in our discipleship.

How often that Great Commandment floats undisturbingly over the heads and out of the hearts of those who hear it. We have to help people recognize the commandment for the hard saying that it is. How can you *command* love? I command you to love one another! That is a hard saying. It is not the syrupy sweet, sentimental saying some people make it seem. I bristle when I hear a TV evangelist say, "God loves you, and so do I." I want to shout back, What do you mean, you love me? You don't even know me!

Saying you love someone and *loving* someone are not the same. Love is not a vague feeling. It is not just a belief that we can love people in general even if we dislike some of them in particular. Nor is it just the acceptance of other people's right to be loved by God. Love is a relationship. It implies a commitment, a willingness to give, to believe, to trust. We cannot escape love's obligations by trying to redefine what Jesus meant by love. "This is my commandment," he said, "that you love one another *as I have loved you.*"

In other words, our love should be like Christ's love. He commands us to love one another in the same way that he has loved us. And how was that? A few verses earlier in that same chapter, Jesus had said, "As the Father has loved me, so have I loved you" (John 15:9). That makes the command even harder. Our love for each other should be like God's love for the Son, not equal but similar, not the same but like it—deeply personal, caring, sacrificial, self-giving, selfless.

That is how Jesus wants us to love each other—with a love so great that we would even be willing to lay down our lives for each other. There is no greater love than that, "for what shall one give," Jesus asked on another occasion, "in return for one's life?" (Matt. 16:26; Mark 8:37). The implication is that you would give everything you have, but that you could never give enough. When Haile Selassie was deposed as emperor of Ethiopia, it was reported that he offered the people who overthrew him his entire fortune, which was said to amount to more than fifteen billion dollars, in exchange for his life and safety.

The love that Christ commands of us extends beyond the bounds of friendship, for he also commanded us to love our enemies. "For if you love those who love you, what reward have you?" (Matt. 5:44, 46). Obeying the command means fulfilling love's demands. This is the point at which evangelistic preaching intersects with prophetic preaching, for it is in the application of the love commandment to all the problems of the world about us that the gospel must be social as well as personal. It is love that constrains us to feed the hungry, clothe the naked, and heal the sick. It is love that moves us to help the poor and liberate the oppressed. It is love that compels us to be peacemakers, justice seekers, and champions of human rights in the world. For the gospel to be truly liberating, it must spring from a heart of love, a love informed by the truth that sets people free (John 8:32).

Here is where evangelism also intersects with liberation theology, which has challenged the church to remember that God has always identified with the poor and the oppressed people of the world. If our gospel is not good news for the poor, what good is it? What good news do we have for a sore-ridden, fly-bitten, starving child in Ethiopia? What is the gospel for those whose basic human rights are denied them by oppressive governments and discriminatory laws?

Evangelism can also join forces with the advocates of liberation theology in acknowledging the corporate dimension of human sin and the corresponding need for a redemption that is corporate and social as well as individual and personal. No one is free unless and until all are free. The gospel we preach must call for the redemption of societies as well as of souls, of systems as well as of persons.

Again, evangelism and liberation theology agree that proclamation without performance is an inadequate expression of the gospel. There must be orthopraxy as well as orthodoxy. Evangelism, therefore, must be more than pious platitudes. Evangelical words must be backed by righteous deeds. We have the liberation theologians to thank for insisting on the integrity of the church's proclamation of the gospel. We may not agree with those liberationists who advocate the use of violence, but we can surely agree with their emphasis on good works, on the corporate dimension of sin and salvation, and the need to address the gospel to the poor. That, after all, was the ministry of our Lord, who in his initial appearance in the synagogue of Nazareth very deliberately chose to read these words from the book of Isaiah:

> The Spirit of the Lord is upon me,
> because he has anointed me
>   to preach good news to the poor.
> He has sent me to proclaim release to the captives
> and recovering of sight to the blind,
> to set at liberty those who are oppressed,
> to proclaim the acceptable year of the Lord.
>   (Luke 4:18–19)

When he had finished reading, as all eyes were upon him, Jesus closed the book, gave it to the attendant, and announced, "Today this scripture has been fulfilled in your hearing" (Luke 4:21).

Jesus laid down his life, not just for his friends but for his enemies as well. He took upon himself the guilt of their sins, and as he hung on the cross he prayed for those who had nailed him to it, and for all who ever betrayed or denied him, before or since. "Father, forgive them; for they know not what they do" (Luke 23:34). There is no greater love, nor will there ever be, than that. We cannot match Jesus' love, but we can imitate it. We cannot equal his love, but we can express it in our lives, by trying to keep his commandment. Most of us will never be called upon to make the supreme sacrifice, but we can make *some* sacrifice. The only way to become a loving person is to start doing what love demands. We cannot make ourselves love, but we can do loving deeds. That is the least we can do, if we call ourselves disciples of Jesus Christ.

Evangelistic preaching cannot ignore or fail to emphasize the gospel demand to love. It is, as Paul declared, "the fulfilling of the law" (Rom. 13:10). God is love and that is good news! Let us, therefore, love one another.

The Great Commission. Another Therefore is the Great Commission: "All authority in heaven and on earth has been given to me," asserted Jesus. "Go therefore and make disciples of all nations" (Matt. 28:19). The Great Commandment to love cannot be separated from the Great Commission to go. They are two sides of the same coin, for love constrains us to preach the gospel, and the gospel we preach is a gospel of love. It is expressed in words and deeds that reflect the love, mercy, justice, and righteousness of Jesus Christ.

God has always been a mission-minded God, whose servants are called to be God's witnesses in and to the world about them, as we see in God's word to the people of Israel: "I have given you as a covenant to the people, a light to the nations, to open the eyes that are blind, to bring out the prisoners from the dungeon" (Isa. 42:6–7). God's servants are God's witnesses, and their witness is to be God's servants. " 'You are my witnesses,' says the Lord, 'and my servant whom I have chosen' " (Isa. 43:10).

In Mark's version of the Great Commission, Jesus charges his disciples, "Go into all the world and preach the gospel to the whole creation" (Mark 16:15), and in the Gospel of Luke he tells them, "Repentance and forgiveness of sins should be preached in his name to all nations, beginning from Jerusalem. You are witnesses to these things" (Luke 24:47–48). Again, as he is parting with them for the very last time, Jesus commissions his disciples to be his witnesses, saying, "You shall receive power when the Holy Spirit has come upon you; and you shall be my witnesses in Jerusalem and in all Judea and Samaria and to the end of the earth" (Acts 1:8).

Across the centuries the Holy Spirit has continued to empower and send out those who are called to be disciples of Jesus Christ. In the words of the apostle Paul, "We are ambassadors for Christ, God making his appeal through us" (2 Cor. 5:20). Bearing witness to Jesus Christ is a vital task, without which the gospel cannot be transmitted from one generation to the next. It is one that must be done with the highest integrity, for, as Paul reminds us, "we are not, like so many, peddlers of God's word; but as persons of sincerity, as commissioned by God, in the sight of God we speak in Christ" (2 Cor. 2:17).

In our evangelistic preaching we must do more, therefore, than merely proclaim the good news. We must remind people of their responsibility to do the same. The Great Commission is for all believers. We have a mandate from our Lord to be his witnesses. Not everyone is gifted to be an evangelist but we are all witnesses, whether we want to be or not. The question is, What kind of witnesses are we going to be? We witness with our lives as well as with our words. Either one without the other is incomplete and inadequate.

Not everyone is an evangelist in the sense that Paul urged Timothy to be (2 Tim. 4:5), but there is something everyone can do to help the *church* evangelize. We have to help each other discover our spiritual gifts and special talents and then use them in the church's evangelistic ministry.

The Great Commission and the Great Commandment are imperatives, not options. They are the explicit demands of the gospel, directed to those who claim to have received it and to those who are thinking of embracing it. They are the Therefores of the Christian gospel, the obligations that every person assumes who confesses Jesus Christ as personal Lord and Savior.

11

Prizing
the Pulpit

Before concluding this study of the pastor-evangelist as preacher, I want to say something about our attitude toward the task of preaching. We can take our cue from Jesus, who told his disciples, "Let us go on to the next towns, that I may preach there also; for that is why I came out" (Mark 1:38). Jesus came to preach, and he commissioned his disciples to do the same. "He called the twelve together," wrote Luke, "and gave them power and authority over all demons and to cure diseases, and he sent them out to preach the kingdom of God and to heal" (Luke 3:1–2).

The Greek word that has been translated "to preach" in these passages is *kēryssein,* which literally means "to cry or proclaim as a herald." It "does not mean the delivery of a learned and edifying or hortatory discourse in well-chosen words and a pleasant voice. It is the declaration of an event. Its true sense is 'to proclaim.'[33] . . . His proclamation is itself event. What he declares takes place in the moment of its declaration."[34]

The disciples are sent out by Jesus to proclaim the same message as their Lord: "Repent, the kingdom of God is at hand!" The heart of the kerygma is the reign of God. "Preaching is not a lecture on the nature of God's kingdom. It is proclamation, the declaration of an event," and "it must be proclaimed again and again, not just to the world, but to the community. . . . If preaching is true proclamation in which God is at work, so that his rule is a reality, then signs and wonders occur. . . . Christian preaching does not per-

suade the hearers by beautiful or clever words. . . . It takes
place in the spirit and in power. It is thus efficacious."[35]

How sad it is when for some the ministry becomes more
of a career than a calling. Their lives are governed by the
worldly measures of success, and they plan their careers
accordingly. Upward mobility means a bigger church and a
better salary. They aspire to occupy some prestigious pulpit,
where their pronouncements will be received as from an
oracle.

What an insidious disease an unhealthy ambition can
become, and none of us preachers is immune to it! The pulpit
is not a prize to be sought but a privilege to be valued. In that
sense we should prize (value) whatever pulpit we may
occupy. It is an awesome thing to speak for God. Preaching
is a sacred trust, the awareness of which is enough to make
one mount the steps to any pulpit with a sense of unworthi-
ness and awe.

The Importance of Preaching

The validity of preaching as a form of communication was
brought home to me by an experience I had in a church where
I served as interim preacher for several months. At the end
of that period, before the new pastor arrived on the scene,
the congregation had a farewell for me on my final Sunday
in the pulpit. There was nothing unusual about that, but what
impressed me about that day was the assumed familiarity of
the parishioners, whose hugs and handshakes were accompanied by verbal expressions of genuine friendship and love,
despite the fact that I did not know the names of most of
them. Our only relationship was that which had developed
between the pulpit and the pew. Other than that, there had
been very little personal contact between me and most of the
people. They knew me only as a preacher, yet they delighted
in introducing me to their relatives and guests that day as
"my good friend." Never again will I question the importance of preaching as a medium of communication. If that
kind of relationship can be established without any other

contact, how much more valuable the preaching ministry becomes when the relationship is augmented by all of the other aspects of pastoral care.

Yet it is a rare preacher who at some time or other has not wondered if her or his preaching is making any impact at all on the people who listen to it Sunday after Sunday. "The appropriate emblem for the pulpit is a big, flapping tongue," said one discouraged pastor in a recent workshop. "If I drew a cartoon of myself, it would look like a great big mouth with arms and legs," said another.

Some have disparaged preaching as the least effective form of communication. "There's nothing duller than a moralistic monologue," a cynic might say. "All you get from the pulpit is one-way communication." To the extent that preaching is moralistic, judgmental, and condemnatory, the cynics have a point. Those we lambaste from the protective ramparts of our pulpit castles have no way of defending themselves against our sermonic spears and arrows. Their momentary defensive strategy is to stop listening. Their round will come when they can go home and have roast minister for dinner. One dejected pastor is said to have complained that the only menu his congregation ever served him was cold shoulder, hot tongue, bitter pills, and sour grapes. Maybe the pastor's preaching warranted such a diet.

I do not know many pastors who deny the importance of preaching, even if they are discouraged by the perceived results of their own preaching ministry. They know that preaching is important not because of the words they speak but because of the Word to whom they bear witness. Their authority derives not from their own wisdom but from their conformity to the will of God. Their preaching is important because they have been called by God to preach. That call was confirmed by the church at their ordination. They have been granted the right to speak; they must earn the right to be heard.

We have won the right to be heard when we are perceived as having authority, the authority of God. In the New Testament the Greek word *exousia* reflects the sovereignty

of God in all things. Nothing occurs apart from the authority
(exousia) of God. The authority of human beings is delegated
authority. "This power cannot be used arbitrarily; in its
application the apostle is bound to his Lord."[36] It cannot be
assumed; it can only be received. It is sometimes synony-
mous with the Greek word *dynamis,* meaning "power."

The church needs women and men who can speak with
that kind of authority and be heard by people who are
desperately yearning for meaning in this chaotic and violent
world in which we live. The authority with which the church
must speak is different from other kinds of authority,
whether political, scientific, social, or military. It is a moral
and spiritual authority, which is listened to because it reflects
the wisdom and justice and righteousness of God. That is the
challenging responsibility to which all ministers of the Word
are called and for which they are ordained.

The Authority of Jesus

The Gospel writers said of Jesus that he taught as one
having *exousia,* not as the scribes—an interesting comment,
in view of the fact that the scribes were supposed to be the
authorities. They were the professional interpreters and
teachers of the Mosaic law, the religious experts, whose
decisions became the oral law of Judaism. Yet the Gospels
draw a clear distinction between the teaching of Jesus and
that of the scribes, saying *he* taught as one having authority.
The difference was not that he was a better teacher. Jesus'
authority lay not in his teaching ability, although he was
indeed a master of the art. The difference was in the *basis* of
his authority. For the scribes, the foundation of their
authority was their knowledge of tradition; for Jesus, it was
his knowledge of God. The authority of the scribes was
based on what others had said before them; the authority of
Jesus was based on his own relationship to God. The scribes
taught *by* authority; Jesus taught *with* authority. That was
the difference.

But many did not perceive it. His own people rejected him. "Where did this man get all this?" they asked. "Is not this the carpenter, the son of Mary?" (Mark 6:2, 3). We know him—that's Mary's boy! In every crowd there were those who resented his words, those who would not accept his authority. The reason was that they applied the wrong test. He had to come from the right town, have the right education, and associate with the right kind of people, in order to be accepted. What seminary did he attend? Who ordained him? So they debated his authority on the basis of how many miracles he produced, and whether he did them openly or secretly, whether his teachings conformed to the traditions of the scribes, and whether the religious authorities believed in him.

Some said, "He is a good man," but others accused him of leading the people astray (John 7:12). Some said, "This is the Christ!" but others said, "Is the Christ to come from Galilee?" (John 7:41). Some said, "When the Christ appears, will he do more signs than this man has done?" (John 7:31), but others were offended by the works he did. When the chief priests and the Pharisees asked the officers why they had not arrested Jesus, the officers answered, "No man ever spoke like this man!" whereupon the Pharisees said, "Are you led astray, you also? Have any of the authorities or of the Pharisees believed in him?" (John 7:45–48).

By such reasoning as this they tested the authority of Jesus, and by such do many test it today. Because the various standards to which people expect Jesus to conform are by no means uniform, they are prone to conclude that there *is* no test by which we can prove the authority of Jesus. It is a matter of faith, they say.

But that is not what Jesus said. He condemned some of his hearers for their unbelief, and he forthrightly told them that it was possible for anyone to know whether or not his teachings were true. The test was not whether he had had any formal training, but whether or not his teachings were of God. "My teaching is not mine, but his who sent me," he said; "if any one's will is to do God's will, that person shall know whether the teaching is from God or whether I am speaking on my own authority'' (John 7:16–17).

In other words, it is not Jesus who must pass the test, but his hearers. To Pontius Pilate he said, "Every one who is of the truth hears my voice" (John 18:37). He told his antagonists, "Whoever is of God hears the words of God; the reason why you do not hear them is that you are not of God" (John 8:47). To those who are earnestly seeking to know and to do the will of God, Christ's teachings are true. The test of his authority is the sincerity of the people who hear his words. The way to know the truth of Jesus' words is not by debate but by action, not by discussing them but by living them.

This concept of authority has tremendous implications for evangelism. People who say they cannot accept Jesus as their Lord and Savior are probably applying the wrong test. Jesus' point is that if they put God at the center of their lives and let Jesus' teachings about God be their guiding light, they will know him to be the true Son of God. They will realize that Jesus' words are truly from God. "My teaching is not mine," he said, "but his who sent me" (John 7:16). The historical Jesus did not claim to speak on his own authority; his authority was from God. "He who speaks on his own authority seeks his own glory," said Jesus; "but he who seeks the glory of him who sent him is true, and in him there is no falsehood" (John 7:18). Jesus was God's mouthpiece. He came to make known his Father's will, but as the Christ of God he could declare, "All authority [exousia] in heaven and on earth has been given to me" (Matt. 28:18).

What a fantastic claim! Jesus asserts his divinely given authority and power to act. The only way to prove the truth of his claim is to *do* God's will. Then and only then can one know whether or not Jesus' teaching is from God. It is when we are consecrated to the *will* of God that we discover that Jesus' teachings are the *word* of God.

The Authority of the Preacher

But who is to say what Jesus' teachings are? This is the problem of *our* authority. People differ in their interpretations of what Jesus meant by what he said. What, then, is the test of a preacher's authority? We who have been theologically trained and ordained to the ministry of the Word are supposed to be the professional interpreters of the scriptures, the modern-day scribes. The word of God is infallible, but those who interpret it are not. How, then, can we know who speaks the truth? "Beloved, do not believe every spirit," says the writer of 1 John, "but test the spirits to see whether they are of God; for many false prophets have gone out into the world" (1 John 4:1). Here we have the same principle: the test of anyone's authority is one's conformity to the will of God. In order to discern this quality in someone else, however, I myself must be in tune with God. As the saying goes, it takes one to know one.

John has given us a way of identifying the true from the false: "By this you know the Spirit of God," he writes; "every spirit which confesses that Jesus Christ has come in the flesh is of God, and every spirit which does not confess Jesus is not of God" (1 John 4:2–3). That is to say, if one's words and deeds glorify Christ, if one's life is a witness to the living Christ, then that person is of God. But if by what one says and does one denies the reality of Christ, then that person is not of God. That is the test.

All criteria, all standards, all tests by which we measure the authority of a person's words in other areas of life have no bearing in the spiritual realm. It is not a matter of education, or technical knowledge, or ability, or beauty, or wealth, or social status, or political power, or occupational position, or cleverness, or popularity, or charm. The humblest persons can speak as those having authority when the Spirit is in them, because their authority is not their own, but God's.

What a lesson for us preachers! Many if not most of us, like Moses, feel quite inadequate to the task to which we have been called. Our sermons may not be paragons of prose. We may not impress a congregation with our ability to speak. We may not be fluent, or dramatic, or entertaining, but if we preach for the glory of God and not for the praise of people, the encouraging word for us is that then we will speak with authority, an authority not of our own but of God.

We must never forget that it is God who has called us to preach and to bear witness to Jesus Christ. The ordaining body or bishop confers upon us the authority to preach, but it is God who gives authority to our words. Seminary gives us the know-how, but it is God who gives us the power. The test of our authority in the pulpit is our conformity to the will of God, for the ultimate source of our authority is God. Those who listen to us must determine whether we pass the test, and in the determining they too are tested. For if they themselves are seeking to do the will of God, according to Jesus they will know whether or not our teaching and preaching are of God.

Two Injunctions

Preaching is a sacred trust and a holy task. If we truly prize the pulpit, therefore, we will value the importance of preaching, and we will heed two injunctions. Here is the first.

Never betray the trust. Our sermons may not be the best, but they should be our own. Some preachers are not as careful as they should be about crediting their sources. There have been some notorious instances of plagiarism, the exposés of which have always been a great embarrassment to the perpetrators as well as a betrayal of their sacred trust as preachers. There is something horribly incongruous about a purloined gospel. The pastor-evangelist should be suffi-ciently imbued with and excited about the good news not to have to steal another's presentation of it. To share the wisdom of others is entirely appropriate, so long as the source is acknowledged. The caveat would not apply to matters of general knowledge or material that is in the public domain.

Plagiarism is a betrayal of trust, and so is insincerity. If it is true that people want to believe that we preachers really believe what we say, shame on us if we ever urge others to embrace a belief we ourselves do not hold! Sincerity is not to be equated with truth; we can be as sincerely wrong as right. But insincerity is always wrong, because it is hypocrisy. The worn-out joke about the cynic who complained that there are too many hypocrites in the church, to which the reply is, "Well, there's always room for one more!" does not apply to preachers. There's no room in the pulpit for hypocrites. To be mistaken in our convictions may be irritating to our hearers, but to be insincere is a betrayal of their trust. They have a right to expect us to believe the gospel we preach, and we have a duty to preach the gospel we believe.

Sincere people can become stubborn, unfortunately, and stubborn people can become arrogant. When sincerity leads to arrogance, that too is a betrayal of the sacred trust of preaching. It is to mistake one's own convictions for truth, and to close one's mind and heart to what the Spirit wants to say to the church. Some preachers sound as if they are speaking *as* God instead of *for* God. This is the temptation of some self-styled prophets who pride themselves on their fearless stands on controversial issues. They forget that to be a true prophet is not a self-conscious choice but a call of God. The initiative is God's, not the preacher's. The call to prophesy should catch us by surprise. For the Hebrew prophets, the responsibility to speak for God was a heavy load to bear. (The Hebrew word for prophecy is *massa,* which means "a burden.") Ian Macpherson, in his book *The Burden of the Lord,* describes the preaching burden as fourfold: the burden of eternity, the burden of sinfulness, the burden of souls, and the burden of the Lord (preaching Christ faithfully). "Where there is no burden," Macpherson declares, "there is no blessing."[37] When some preachers claim to be prophetic, they are more arrogant than biblical. They need to remember what the sage said long ago: "Every one who is arrogant is an abomination to the LORD" (Prov. 16:5).

If thinking of oneself too highly is a betrayal of the preaching trust, so is thinking of one's role not highly enough. The arrogant preacher usurps the divine glory; the indolent preacher shirks the human responsibility. To be slothful about one's preaching responsibility is to deny its importance. Congregations have the right to expect their pastors not to *be* the best, but to *do* their best. Anything less is unacceptable. That is true no matter what the size of the congregation may be. Whether we are preaching to twenty persons or two hundred or two thousand, pastor-evangelists approach the task of preaching with the same conscientious preparation, the same sense of urgency, the same awareness of the importance of proclaiming faithfully the word of God. Be the hearers of high or low station, rich or poor, young or old, they all deserve our very best effort. To do less is to betray the sacred trust. It is also a violation of the second injunction, which follows.

Never neglect the task. For most pastors, it is not laziness that tempts them to neglect their preaching ministry. On the contrary, it is the very opposite of indolence. The struggle of a conscientious pastor to keep up with the ceaseless demands of a busy parish can wreak havoc on a well-intentioned schedule of sermon preparation. Other aspects of pastoral care often must take precedence over the time a pastor has set aside for reading and study, not to mention personal devotions. Nevertheless, the pastor-evangelist, knowing the importance of the preaching ministry, resolves never to neglect that holy task, for preaching is an important part of pastoral care. Our preaching should always be informed by and related to the needs of our people.

There is no easy solution to the problem of time and no set rules for managing it. Pastors differ in temperament, stamina, life-style, and personality, not to mention family and social obligations, spiritual gifts and talents, other pastoral demands, stewardship priorities, theological viewpoints, work habits, and commitment to people. Everyone must decide individually what schedule seems to work best, allowing for the flexibility that congregational life demands. We cannot schedule emergencies or expect people to die at our convenience. One of my students, during a class discussion on how, as a pastor, one should schedule time for pastoral counseling, asserted, "I intend to tell the congregation shortly after I arrive that I will not tolerate anyone who calls me at home after eight o'clock in the evening," to which another student retorted, "Don't worry, you won't have any calls!"

I should hope that the polity of your church provides for your freedom in the pulpit. No one else should be able to tell you what to preach or how to preach. That is your calling, your right and your responsibility as a minister of the Word. For that reason, though you may absent yourself from the pulpit from time to time, you should never abandon it. If the preaching ministry is your responsibility, you are obligated to see that whoever takes over during your absence is a worthy substitute. Many a pastor has been embarrassed by an insensitive guest preacher who has rushed in where angels fear to tread and stirred up a hornets' nest in the process. Usually it is an unwitting faux pas, perhaps simply a matter of poor timing, as when a guest preacher decided to preach on the text, "And we all, with unveiled face, beholding the glory of the Lord, are being changed into his likeness" (2 Cor. 3:18). The sermon topic was "It's Time for a Change!" That seems innocent enough, except for the fact that the first notice in the church bulletin that Sunday read, "Next Tuesday marks Rev. Smith's thirty-ninth anniversary as pastor of Central Church." (The names have been changed to protect the guilty!)

It is especially important not to abandon the pulpit when on occasion you invite a layperson to preach. These people are always grateful for whatever assistance you offer them by way of suggesting possible topics and texts, making available to them your commentaries and other resources, discussing any theological questions they may have, editing their manuscript, and helping them with their delivery. It is not a matter of imposing upon or interfering with them but of making yourself available to them. Far from feeling threatened or resentful, they will welcome your tactful suggestions. Not only will they be relieved of some anxiety, they will also appreciate better the careful and serious way you go about the task of preaching Sunday by Sunday. It is a marvelous teaching experience for the pastor-evangelist, as well as a unique opportunity for faith sharing. If there are moments when people are especially receptive to the gospel, this is certainly one of them.

We have been talking about prizing the pulpit. Although everything that has been said in this chapter applies to the preaching ministry in general, it has special relevance for the pastor-evangelist, who feels the same constraint the apostle Paul did to proclaim the good news of Jesus Christ. "Woe to me," cried Paul, "if I do not preach the gospel!" (1 Cor. 3:16).

And woe to us if we do not do the same!

Appendix A
The Integrity of Evangelism

This address was given on the occasion of my inauguration to the Ashenfelter Chair of Ministry and Evangelism at Princeton Theological Seminary, September 21, 1980. (Salutations and other introductory remarks have been omitted.)

I thought long and hard about my topic for tonight. Realizing that in a single address I could not do justice to two such comprehensive subjects as ministry and evangelism, and feeling that you might be more interested in what someone would have to say about evangelism than about ministry, I decided to focus on the former. I hope, however, that what I am going to say is applicable to ministry in general.

My remarks are not intended to make a case for a Chair of Evangelism at Princeton Seminary. Nor is it my intention to advocate a method for teaching evangelism to seminary students. Rather I want to discuss what I consider to be the fundamentals of integrity for those who teach, or practice, or even talk about evangelism in the church, or on the campus, or wherever. This address could be titled "The ABCs of Evangelistic Integrity," because the letters stand for three words which summarize the content of that integrity.

The first word is *awareness*. Most of us are aware that evangelism is a controversial subject. It is controversial because some people confuse their definition of evangelism with their concept of method, the meaning with the means. They are opposed to evangelism because they don't like the way some people do it, so they throw out the baby with the bathwater.

We who teach or talk about evangelism need to be aware of that confusion, lest we contribute to it instead of helping to dispel it. We need to realize that there is an appropriate evangelistic style for every time and place, and the challenge is to know how to relate the approach to the setting, how to coordinate the medium and the message.

But what is evangelism? The Church of England's Commission on Evangelism adopted this classic definition in 1918 and reaffirmed it in 1945, and it has been widely used ever since: "To evangelize is so to present Christ Jesus in the power of the Holy Spirit, that [people] shall come to put their trust in God through him, to accept him as their Saviour and serve him as their King in the fellowship of his Church."[38]

The question is not whether to evangelize or not to evangelize; that question has been answered for us by the mandate of Jesus Christ himself, who has commissioned us to go and make disciples of all nations and be his witnesses to the ends of the earth. We have been reminded of that commission over and over again in the mandates laid upon their constituents by just about every denomination and council of churches, including the Roman Catholic Church.

The Governing Board of the National Council of Churches adopted unanimously a policy statement which declared evangelism to be "a primary function of the church in its congregational, denominational, and ecumenical manifestations."

In a document entitled "A Theological Reflection on the Work of Evangelism," the Division of Studies of the World Council of Churches stated, "The basic urgency of evangelism arises . . . from the nature and content of the gospel itself, and its authority lies in the recognition by all believers that they have been claimed by Christ precisely for the purpose of becoming his witnesses."[39] In another document on "The Missionary Task of the Church," the World Council affirmed that Christians are bound to confront all people with the decision to commit themselves to Jesus Christ.

Deeply concerned about the alarming decline in membership, the 188th General Assembly of the United Presbyterian Church approved the report of a special committee calling upon each congregation to study its own patterns of membership and formulate specific plans of action. The following year, the 189th General Assembly reaffirmed the belief that "God's saving love in Jesus Christ includes all people" and acknowledged the church's responsibility to share that good news in word and deed with people everywhere.[40]

Year after year the General Assembly has called upon Presbyterian churches to give top priority to evangelism. Other denominations have issued similar mandates to their member congregations. So the question is not *whether* but *how* to evangelize, and for thoughtful Christians that means how to evangelize with integrity. For we are aware of the dangers of the resurgence of a hyperconservative, evangelical aggressiveness too often characterized by a superficial, pietistic, literalistic, judgmental, insensitive, atheological, anti-intellectual, irrelevant, obscurantist style of evangelism.

Integrity demands that we be aware of these dangers and avoid them. We live in a pluralistic world, where the truth claims of other religions and philosophies are sounding loud and clear, and we cannot act as if there are no other appeals than ours for human hearts and minds, or that God listens only to Christian prayers, as the President of the Southern Baptist Convention stated recently. We can have our Christian beliefs and express them with conviction, but we won't win many followers for Christ with an arrogant, holier-than-thou attitude, like the would-be evangelists who distributed Christian literature in the parking lot and vestibule of a New Jersey synagogue during a service. The rabbi was justifiably indignant, when he wrote in an article entitled "Cry, Little Jesus," from a song he had once heard, "Is this Christianity? Is this Christian ethics—to sneak into a synagogue and disseminate the word of Jesus? If it is, then cry, little Jesus, for there is much to cry about. Cry, little Jesus, for your followers who think that their God could sanction such devious methods of propagating the faith. Cry, little Jesus, for those who invoke your name while stooping to new lows in spreading your gospel. Cry, little Jesus, for sick souls who are out to capture Jewish souls, to seduce the followers of Moses in a Jewish house of worship and a darkened parking lot."[41]

What a message for Yom Kippur! That incident occurred several years ago. More recently Jews have themselves become "evangelistic." "Judaism from birth has been a missionary religion," Rabbi Alexander Schindler, President of the Union of American Hebrew Congregations, representing 750 Reform temples, was quoted as saying by *Newsweek* magazine. "Abraham was a missionary. We ought to resume our time-honored tradition."[42] Conservative Rabbi Marc Tannenbaum of the American Jewish Committee agreed, commenting in the same article that "the Jewish people have a moral obligation to testify to the truths, values and life-styles that Judaism uniquely provides."

The reality of this development was brought home to me when a member of a Conservative synagogue showed up for an evangelism seminar that I conducted at the Center of Continuing Education here at Princeton. A very intelligent woman with a Ph.D. in social psychology, she explained that her reason for attending was to learn the techniques of Christian evangelism and take them back to her synagogue. Since then we have become pen pals, and her letters have been sometimes bitterly frank. Here is a sample: "I say you are selling false doctrine. You [Christians] love Jesus, not God, the God of Abraham, Isaac, and Jacob, whom Christians call their 'spiritual father.' Indeed, I felt a sadness, even envy, thinking, If all that love and tenderness for Jesus were meant for the Reality, God! For the 1800 years of false witness Christianity has brought against Judaism, started by the Jew Saul, I, this Jew, hold that Christian worship of the Jew Jesus is a form of Baal-worship, idolatry; and in God's good time and grace, it will cease."

Evangelistic integrity demands an awareness that we live in a society where such feelings exist, where religious tolerance is considered a virtue and most people have an antipathy toward imposing their beliefs on others, where enlightened spirits are calling for interfaith dialogue, and ecumenism means more than a merger of several Protestant denominations. An ecumenical temper, wrote David Stowe, former Executive Officer of the Division of Overseas Ministries of the National Council of Churches, "welcomes relationships with others of diverse points of view . . . and this almost necessarily implies a degree of tentativeness about one's own particular expression of faith."[43]

But there is still the mandate. So we are faced with the challenge of knowing how to fulfill the Great Commission while espousing the right of people to worship or not to worship as they please, how to bear witness in a pluralistic society, how to be both evangelistic and ecumenical at the same time. There are many other challenges of which we must also be aware, such as those imposed upon us by linguistic analysis, which questions the meaningfulness of God-language, and logical positivism, which challenges the validity of any statement that cannot be verified or falsified by empirical evidence. Average unchurched Americans may never have heard of linguistic analysis or logical positivism, but they think in those categories. They don't understand our language games, and they don't accept our truth claims.

Add to those the challenges of secular humanism, materialism, communism, and other ideologies, superstitions like astrology, religious cults, psychological fads, the electronic church, the Playboy-Playgirl philosophy, and all the other influences with which would-be evangelists must compete, plus the innumerable problems with which our faith must cope, such as nuclear power, toxic waste, the arms race, poverty, world hunger, political corruption, pollution, inflation, the energy crisis, the rehabilitation of Asian, Hispanic, and other refugees, unemployment, racial injustice, international terrorism, crime, violence, the Moral Majority and the immoral minority, to mention just a few, all of which underscore the immensity of our educational task. We who are teaching future ministers must realize that the integrity of their witness in the world will depend first of all upon their realistic *awareness* of the kind of world it is. It is up to us to prepare them to accept the mandate of Christ and the church, and of the world that awaits them outside these walls.

That calls also for *balance,* which is the second basic ingredient of the integrity of evangelism—and, indeed, of ministry in general. As a former pastor, I can testify to the need for integrating the theological disciplines with the practice of ministry. This is the cry of most seminary graduates, who in their first two weeks in the parish inevitably encounter situations for which they feel ill prepared. What did I, as a recent seminary graduate, know about ministering in a predominantly Jewish community? Or about training evangelistic callers? Or about organizing a stewardship commitment campaign? Or about renovating a church? No one had told me what to do when the president of the Board of Trustees informed me that the pastor was not permitted to attend their meetings.

But I never blamed the seminary for such omissions, and I did not feel unprepared, because I had been given the basic tools for ministry and I had learned to think theologically. I realized that no matter how practical my professors might have tried to make my courses, they could never anticipate every situation that might arise. Nor did I ever think that was their task. It is important, nevertheless, for a seminary to try to integrate the practical and the classical dimensions of theological education. That's why we have a Department of Practical Theology, one of whose functions is to do just that. To be sure, it is a function in which the other departments share, as each professor sees opportunities to relate his or her discipline to the practice of ministry. Obviously, that is more easily done in some disciplines than in others.

What is called for is balance. The age-old debate between those who perceive a seminary to be a graduate school of religion and those who see it as a professional school is perpetuating an unfortunate dichotomy. A seminary cannot allow itself to be one or the other, but somehow must strive to be both. As one who spent sixty semester hours in a graduate school of religion at a major university, I know the difference. It was not easy to apply what I was studying to the practical demands of the pastorate. In the midst of typing one of my term papers, my exasperated secretary expressed her frustration with my theological jargon, threatening that if I ever used that kind of language in the pulpit, she would leave the church!

This illustrates an important task of ministry, which is that of constantly trying to elevate the level of people's theological competence, their appreciation of sacred music, their understanding of stewardship, their commitment to the church, the quality of their discipleship, their moral sensitivity, their social awareness, and every other aspect of their spiritual lives, *without losing touch with where they are*. The wise shepherd never runs too far ahead of the flock. We who teach must help our students to develop the skills to do this, the ability to apply theological principles to practical situations. We must help them to see how their theology informs and illumines and determines their ministry.

But the *onus* is not entirely *on us* as teachers. For the principle of balance applies also to students, who in their understandable demand for the practical skills must not lose sight of their need for theological competence. In their impatience to get out into the real world, too many students fail to appreciate the fantastic opportunity afforded them by their three years at seminary. Many will never again have the same chance for such an extended period of theological reflection and serious, disciplined study. It is extremely difficult to claim and to carve out the time for concentrated study amid the demands and pressures of the parish ministry. The wise student will take advantage of these precious years and enjoy them while he or she can. It is the proper balance of practical skill and sound theology that will give integrity to one's ministry, and especially to one's evangelistic efforts, which are part of one's ministry.

You and I may not consider ourselves evangelists, but we must find those who have the gift and equip them to do the evangelist's work. That is a task which calls for awareness and for balance. Consider the relationship between evangelism and social action. The personal salvationists and the social activists are still at each other's throats. They argue about another false dichotomy. The relationship between evangelism and social action is not either/or but both/and. Although it should be obvious, I have learned never to take it for granted that the both/and relationship is understood and accepted, especially by those who are inclined to stress one side over against the other. We who teach should not permit the dichotomy—which, though real, is wrong—to go unchallenged, whenever we encounter it.

An evangelistic approach that is truly concerned with reaching the whole person cannot overlook the social dimension of a person's life or the context in which a person's life is lived. The love of Christ constrains us to be concerned about the needs of others, and that concern can and does involve us in the struggle for human justice, freedom, and peace—not only as individuals but as churches.

I am aware that what I have said violates some of the principles of the Church Growth Movement, which sees social action as a barrier to growth. Its advocates cite Dean Kelley's excellent sociological study, *Why Conservative Churches Are Growing*[44] in support of this view. Kelley would have preferred to refer to them as strict churches rather than conservative churches, but that is one more example of editorial prerogative. Churches cease to grow, says Kelley, when they depart from their central purpose, which is to answer the human quest for meaning. I do not doubt the accuracy of the statement. It is the accession to it and the use of it which is one of my points of contention with the Church Growth Movement—that, and the homogeneous unit principle. Donald McGavran's observation that people "like to become Christians without crossing racial, linguistic, or class barriers"[45] is undoubtedly true, but does that mean that churches should therefore seek only their own kind? "Of all the scientific hypotheses developed within the Church Growth framework, this one as nearly as any approaches a law," writes C. Peter Wagner.[46]

The Church Growth advocates are echoing what Gibson Winter pointed out more than twenty years ago in his book *The Suburban Captivity of the Churches,* which was a penetrating sociological analysis of the exodus of the mainline white churches from the city to suburbia. Whereas the mark of the primitive church was social inclusiveness—rich and poor, Jew and Gentile, slave and free—the characteristic of the church of the metropolis is exclusiveness, based largely upon economic status. "A few highbrows and a few lowbrows can be thrown into a congregational mix, but the core group has to be drawn from similar occupational, income group, educational level, ethnic background, and residential level if the congregation is to survive," wrote Professor Winter. The key to Protestant churchgoing is the search by middle-class people for socially homogeneous groupings, and the key to homogeneity is the economic level. "A Protestant congregation collapses when it cannot recruit a socially homogeneous membership."[47]

My contention with the Church Growth Movement's proponents is that whereas Gibson Winter rued the fact of congregational homogeneity, they are advocating it as an evangelistic principle. And whereas Dean Kelley appealed for churches to show their members how their social causes fit in with their meaning system, the Church Growth people advocate minimal if any involvement by the church in social action. "To the degree that socially involved churches become engaged in social action, as distinguished from social service, they can expect church growth to diminish," says Peter Wagner.[48]

By no means do I intend to imply by what I have said that church growth is not a legitimate emphasis, even a valid priority for every congregation. My concern is for the integrity of evangelism, which should be color-blind and class-blind. Awareness does not permit us to deny the way things are, but balance demands that we question whether that's the way things ought to be. Our evangelistic call is not to be homogeneous congregations but to be faithful disciples of Jesus Christ, not to seek first the people like us but to seek first the kingdom of God and his righteousness, not to be the community's most successful organization but to be Christ's servant community. The people of Israel were called not to indulge their chosen status but to be God's faithful witnesses to the nations, and we Christians are called not only to relate to those with whom we feel comfortable but to follow where the Lord of the church leads us.

Do we not still believe that the love of Jesus Christ can transcend the barriers that separate us one from another? Has he not broken down the dividing walls of hostility? As long as there are segregated neighborhoods, there will be segregated churches; and as long as there are segregated churches, there will be segregated neighborhoods. The need is for inclusive congregations with pluralistic programs in which many different kinds of people can find meaning and fulfillment. The evangelistic challenge is not to ignore or deny our racial, social, or class differences but by the grace of Christ to transcend them.

The integrity of evangelism in a pluralistic society calls for a balanced theology, as well as a balanced program. I am not suggesting that there should not be traditional emphases or denominational differences; I am appealing for a theology that attempts to present the whole gospel, not a one-sided version of it. Whenever there ceases to be a proper balance, the seeds of a new sect are sown. Those whose ultimate questions are not dealt with will seek their answers elsewhere.

A pluralistic society calls for a pluralistic church, which means a proper *balance* between the personal and the social gospel, between the traditional and the contemporary in worship, between a unified and a diversified membership, between ethnic identity and spiritual unity, between a pastoral and a prophetic ministry, between outreach and nurture, between proclamation and communication, between evangelism and church renewal, between growth and mission. There is a fine line between wanting the church to grow and making a fetish of church growth, between growth as a means to the end of mission and growth as an end in itself. It behooves us to know the difference, if our evangelism is to have integrity.

But the integrity of evangelism depends not only upon our awareness of the mandate and the balance of our message. It has to do also, and most importantly, with the *credibility* of the messenger. Integrity demands that we get our own faith house in order before we try to win others to Christ. That process should be the number one priority of our seminary experience. What good is a theological education without faith? What good is knowledge without commitment? Is our ministry a career or a calling? If we are not called by God to be ministers, we have no right to be called ministers of God.

Most students come to seminary with a genuine sense of call. They are highly motivated, eager to learn, full of idyllic expectations. But for some the spark sputters and dies, and they drop out of seminary, while others simply cool off. Excitement turns to cynicism, and personal beliefs are buried beneath the books. That's not just a Princeton syndrome. It happens everywhere, to varying degrees. The members of the senior class at one mainline Protestant seminary were asked to complete the Theological Schools Inventory (TSI), a self-evaluation instrument which explores such things as motivation and decision. As a group they felt that both their sense of call and their desire to witness had declined considerably since they entered seminary.

Whatever this says about their seminary experience, it proves that we on the faculty have a pastoral as well as a teaching responsibility to our students. We are here to produce not scholars of religion but religious scholars, men and women of faith *and* knowledge. Is not a seminary a community of faith, and is it not the responsibility of the members of any community of faith to encourage one another's faith? It is the balance between piety and learning for which our Reformed tradition has always stood.

The American Association of Theological Schools has called for instruction that takes seriously the needs of students as persons, the vocation of ministry, and the life and mission of the church. According to AATS, the Master of Divinity program should provide experiences in which students can grow in their personal faith and in their commitment to the practice of ministry. We may send forth from this campus well-educated graduates, but without that personal faith and strong commitment their preaching will have no power, their pastoral ministry no credibility, and their evangelism no integrity. If, as they say, faith is not taught but caught, then we all must be faith carriers. It is as true of teachers as it is of evangelists that the impact of the message depends upon the credibility of the messenger. We lose credibility when our deeds deny our words. As one of the historic Presbyterian principles of church order states, "There is an inseparable connection between faith and practice, truth and duty. Otherwise, it would be of no consequence either to discover truth or to embrace it." David Stowe has reminded us that we need to bridge the credibility gap between what we say and what we do, as individuals and as a witnessing community. Christian proselytizing, divisiveness and competitiveness, said Stowe, are among the biggest reasons for the lack of credibility among people of other religions.[49]

So the credibility of the messenger depends upon the quality of the messenger's faith, and it also depends upon the authority of the messenger's words. They will have authority if they are inspired by, based upon and true to the Word of God, which, as the Presbyterian Confession of 1967 declares, "is spoken to his church today where the Scriptures are faithfully preached and attentively read in dependence on the illumination of the Holy Spirit and with readiness to receive their truth and direction."[50] A credible faith is an informed faith, as well as a sincere faith.

It is also an honest faith. That means admitting one's doubts, not ignoring or denying them. It means recognizing and confessing one's own faith assumptions. If my belief in God depended upon my ability to prove the existence of God, I could no longer believe. Faith is a gift. I cannot make myself believe what I cannot believe. Faith is not something I can make myself have; faith is something I find myself with. I wake up believing, and my faith is confirmed over and over again by my own experience of the God I believe in. God is not a provable fact, but for me God is a verifiable assumption.

Some evangelists lack credibility because they don't seem to recognize that they can't prove the existence of God. I read an article not long ago by a famous radio preacher that was entitled "Seven Proofs God Exists." His arguments are his own improvisations on the Thomistic proofs, all of which presuppose what they claim to prove. The preacher's first proof, for example, is that we live in a universe which is governed by laws. "The existence of LAW," he says, "unchangeable, immutable, irrevocable, unseen and yet active, ABSOLUTELY DEMANDS the existence of a GREAT LAWGIVER! . . . That LAWGIVER is GOD!"[51] So, too, the very existence of life demands a Lifegiver, and the Great Lifegiver is God! Or again, the fact of creation demands a Creator . . . God! Likewise, design in the universe proves the existence of a Designer . . . God! So it goes.

Tautological arguments like these will not convince an intelligent skeptic, and those who use them will lack credibility with hearers who see through them. So will those who use dishonest or manipulative methods to gain their objectives. Success is not sinful, but what some people do to attain it may be. Witness the advice of a well-known newspaper columnist to a pastor wanting to know how to boost attendance: "Name at least three members of your audience [in your sermon] each Sunday [to illustrate or corroborate a point]. . . . Those three who are named in a complimentary fashion naturally are pleased, so they think your sermon is better than usual! And then they contribute more generously, too. But all the other parishioners will also wake up, to look around and see where [so-and-so] is sitting! So everybody is stimulated. . . . And by naming three people relevantly each Sunday, you cover 150 families each year! Speak loudly, if you don't have a microphone. And abhor any overhanging mustache, for the latter obscures much of your lip movements! [Obviously he wasn't thinking about women in ministry.] . . . Inject some appropriate humor to produce a laugh. . . . To obtain three pages of wholesome humor, decent and quite fit for pulpit use, follow what other professional speakers do and subscribe to *Quote,* the weekly magazine full of current brilliant quotations. It is published at Anderson, South Carolina, and ranks next to the Bible and a concordance as the clergyman's [sic] ally! . . . For additional advice, send for my booklet, 'Public Platform Psychology,' enclosing a long, stamped, return envelope, plus 25 cents."[52]

To employ such tactics for those reasons would be sinful, because the methods are manipulative and the motive is insincere. The integrity of evangelism is not based on the cleverness of our gimmicks but on the sincerity of our faith. The best way to strengthen the faith of others is to be an example of faith. Most people don't want a dissertation about God from the pulpit or in the living room; they want a message from a person who really believes in the God she or he is talking about. Our task as evangelists is not to prove that Jesus is the Christ; that we can never do. Our task is to show by the way we speak and act that we believe he is—and *that,* by God's grace, we can do. Credibility is earned not by pretending to be perfect but by being honest about our imperfections and sincere in our desire to be faithful. Our evangelism will have integrity as long as we remember our own limitations and depend upon the Holy Spirit, for the Spirit is the converter of human hearts, not you and I. Whatever we do, therefore, must always be undergirded by prayer.

The awareness of the mandate, the balance of the message, the credibility of the messenger. These, then, are the ABCs of integrity for evangelism, and for all Christian ministry. There are many other letters in the alphabet! The trouble with some of us is that we have forgotten our ABCs.

The story is told of a great admiral, in the days when ships of war were sailing ships, who before every naval battle used to retire to his cabin, where he would take a piece of paper from his desk drawer and sit alone with his head bowed for a few minutes, meditating on what he had read. Then he would go out and take command of the fleet. One of the admiral's greatest admirers was his orderly, who would have given anything to know what wonderful words were written on the piece of paper which so inspired the admiral before each battle. Finally, the orderly's curiosity got the better of him, and at an opportune moment when the admiral was out on deck, the young man slipped into the stateroom and, with trembling hands, opened the paper on which these words were written: "Starboard is right. Port is left."

May God give us grace to remember our ABCs.

Appendix B

Evaluating
Your Church Bulletin

Church Bulletin Checklist

To evaluate your church bulletin as an evangelistic instrument, read each of the following statements. If it is completely true for your bulletin, circle the number at the left. If it is not true or does not apply, do not circle the number; cross it off. The numerical values indicate the item's increasing evangelistic importance on a scale of 1 to 5, with 5 being the most important. (The numbers in parentheses refer to the percent of churches omitting that item from their bulletins; some of these items are listed in chapter 1.)

When you have gone through the list, add the numbers you have circled and compare your total with the appropriate rating scale (with or without Communion). This is not a precise scientific instrument, but it will give you a general picture of the quality and usefulness of your church bulletin as an evangelistic aid. And by studying the statements for which you could *not* circle a number, you can determine areas in which there may be room for improvement.

Church Information

5   The name of the church is indicated on the front, on the back, or at the top of page 2. (1%)
5   The denomination of the church is included on the front, on the back, or at the top of page 2. (5%)
5   The address of the church is indicated on the front or the back. (37%)
2   The zip code is included with the address. (67%)
5   The church telephone number (or the pastor's) is clearly indicated. (52%)
1   The area code is included with the telephone number. (86%)

5   The name(s) of the pastor(s) is(are) indicated on the front or the back. (8%)

2   The names and positions of other full-time and/or part-time staff members (including seminary assistants, if any) are listed. (24%)

Worship Information

4   The date of the service is indicated on the front (or at the top of page 2). (4%)

5   The time(s) of the service(s) is(are) indicated at the top of page 2 (or on the front). (9%)

2   There is an indication of when latecomers may be seated. (48%)

3   There is an indication of when to stand or sit. (26%)

3   The words of all prayers (other than the Lord's Prayer), creeds, and responses, sung or spoken, are included, or the page references are given in the order of worship. (81%)

1   The use of "debts" or "trespasses" in the Lord's Prayer is indicated. (76%)

3   The names of the worship leaders are shown by their respective parts of the service. (63%)

4   The numbers of the hymns are shown. (4%)

1   The first lines of the hymns are shown. (10%)

3   The titles of anthems or special music (if any) are shown. (18%)

1   The titles of the postlude and prelude (if any) are shown. (31%)

2   The names of the ushers are included. (64%)

2   The names of the greeters or fellowship hour hosts and hostesses are included. (55%)

1   The names of the flower donors are included. (27%)

Visitor Information

4   A welcome to visitors is included. (49%)

3   Information about joining and/or an invitation to join the church (Inquirers Classes, etc.) is included in the notes. (76%)

5   A request to sign an attendance pad or guest book, or to fill out a visitor card, is included. (68%)

3   Information about seeking help or any kind of pastoral care is included in the notes. (82%)

2   The sermon topic and text and scripture passages for next
     Sunday are included. (82%)

Program Information

4   A weekly church calendar is included. (41%)
5   Church school times are indicated. (52%)
3   Christian education class offerings for various ages are indi-
     cated. (72%)
2   Nursery hours and services are indicated. (61%)
2   Rehearsal times for the choir(s) are indicated. (49%)
2   Notices of coming special events are included. (27%)

Bulletin Style

3   The type is legible (dark enough and not too small). (4%)
1   The layout is not too "busy" (too much printing per page, too
     crowded). (9%)
4   The Order of Worship is clearly presented (use of indentation,
     spacing, boldface, capitalization, etc.). (9%)
3   There are no mistakes in grammar, syntax, punctuation, or
     spelling. (9%)
1   There are no typographical errors. (7%)
2   The church slogan or statement of mission or purpose is
     included. (79%)
2   There is a picture or sketch of the church on the front cover.
     (49%)

Communion Instructions (if applicable)

4   The Order of Service is clearly indicated (or page references
     given to the prayer book).
4   There is a note indicating who is invited to participate.
2   The note includes instructions regarding the procedure for
     serving the elements.
3   The note includes an explanation as to when the elements
     are to be consumed (As served? After everyone is served?
     etc.).
1   The purpose of the communion offering (if any) is indicated.

RATING SCALE

Without Communion	Rating	With Communion
109–116	Just about perfect!	123–130
101–108	Excellent	115–122
93–100	Very good	107–114
85–92	Good	99–106
77–84	Fair	91–98
69–76	Poor	83–90
68 or below	Very poor	82 or below

Appendix C
Scriptural Reflections
(Childs Memorial Service)

The following reflections were given at the memorial service for my wife's parents, Harwood and Willa Childs, who were killed in an automobile accident on June 7, 1972. The service was held in the then First Presbyterian (now the Nassau Presbyterian) Church of Princeton, New Jersey, where they had been active members for many years.

Death is a teacher from which the believing heart can learn much. How better can we learn that life is a gift, a precious gift which we can never take for granted? When, if not now, can we better understand what the apostle Paul was saying when he wrote to the Christians at Thessalonica:

> As to the times and the seasons, brethren, you have no need to have anything written to you. For you yourselves know well that the day of the Lord will come like a thief in the night. When people say, "There is peace and security," then sudden destruction will come upon them as travail comes upon a woman with child, and there will be no escape. But you are not in darkness, brethren, for that day to surprise you like a thief. For you are all sons of light and sons of the day; we are not of the night or of darkness. . . . Since we belong to the day, let us be sober, and put on the breastplate of faith and love, and for a helmet the hope of salvation. For God has not destined us for wrath, but to obtain salvation through our Lord Jesus Christ, who died for us so that whether we wake or sleep we might live with him. Therefore encourage one another and build one another up, just as you are doing.
>
> (1 Thessalonians 5:1–5, 8–11)

So let us say with the psalmist:

Lord, make me to know mine end.
And the measure of my days, what it is;
That I may know how frail I am.
Behold, thou hast made my days as a handbreadth;
And mine age is as nothing before thee
                                         (Psalm 39:4–5, KJV)

Surely, then, death should teach us gratitude, for when, if not now, do we need more to count our blessings? We who have known the friendship and love of Harwood and Willa Childs have truly been blessed. For they were indeed a most remarkable and unique couple, each one very special to us all.

Many of you have been in their house at 51 Lake Lane, and you know that their home tells its own story of their industry and grace, their cheerfulness and hospitality, their faith and their love. If cleanliness is next to godliness, to be in Willa Childs's home was to be very close to the kingdom of God. She was the kind of wife and mother of whom the ancient sage wrote:

A good wife who can find?
    She is far more precious than jewels.
The heart of her husband trusts in her,
    and he will have no lack of gain.
She does him good, and not harm,
    all the days of her life. . . .
She rises while it is yet night
    and provides food for her household
    and tasks for her maidens. . . .
She opens her hand to the poor,
    and reaches out her hands to the needy. . . .
Strength and dignity are her clothing,
    and she laughs at the time to come.
She opens her mouth with wisdom,
    and the teaching of kindness is on her tongue.
She looks well to the ways of her household,
    and does not eat the bread of idleness.
Her children rise up and call her blessed;
    her husband also, and he praises her:
"Many women have done excellently,
    but you surpass them all."
Charm is deceitful, and beauty is vain,
    but a woman who fears the Lord is to be praised.

Give her of the fruit of her hands,
and let her works praise her in the gates.
(Proverbs 31, selected verses)

Willa Childs had all these qualities and many more. Hers was a
strong faith. How well she who loved the birds and the flowers
could understand the teachings of Jesus:

Look at the birds of the air: they neither sow nor reap nor
gather into barns, and yet your heavenly Father feeds them.
Are you not of more value than they? And which of you by
being anxious can add one cubit to his span of life? And why
are you anxious about clothing? Consider the lilies of the field,
how they grow; they neither toil nor spin; yet I tell you, even
Solomon in all his glory was not arrayed like one of these. But
if God so clothes the grass of the field, which today is alive and
tomorrow is thrown into the oven, will he not much more
clothe you, O you of little faith? Therefore, do not be anxious,
saying, "What shall we eat?" or "What shall we drink?" or
"What shall we wear?" For the Gentiles seek all these things;
and your heavenly Father knows that you need them all. But
seek first his kingdom and his righteousness, and all these
things shall be yours as well.

(Matthew 6:26–33)

Like Paul, she could say:

I coveted no one's silver or gold. . . . You yourselves know
that these hands ministered to my necessities, and to those who
were with me. In all things I have shown you that by so toiling
one must help the weak, remembering the words of the Lord
Jesus, how he said, "It is more blessed to give than to
receive."

(Acts 20:33–35)

Will she not be at the right hand of the King to hear him say:

"Come, O blessed of my Father, inherit the kingdom prepared
for you from the foundation of the world; for I was hungry and
you gave me food, I was thirsty and you gave me drink, I was
a stranger and you welcomed me, I was naked and you clothed
me, I was sick and you visited me, I was in prison and you came
to me." Then the righteous will answer him, "Lord, when did
we see thee hungry and feed thee, or thirsty and give thee

drink? And when did we see thee a stranger and welcome thee, or naked and clothe thee? And when did we see thee sick or in prison and visit thee?" And the King will answer them, "Truly, I say to you, as you did it to one of the least of these my brethren, you did it to me."

(Matthew 25:34–40)

How grateful we are for a life like that of Willa Childs, and for a life like that of her husband, who truly fits the psalmist's portrait of a godly man:

O Lord, who shall sojourn in thy tent?
　Who shall dwell on thy holy hill?
He who walks blamelessly, and does what is right,
　and speaks truth from his heart;
who does not slander with his tongue,
　and does no evil to his friend,
　nor takes up a reproach against his neighbor;
in whose eyes a reprobate is despised,
　but who honors those who fear the Lord;
who swears to his own hurt and does not change. . . .
He who does these things shall never be moved.

(Psalm 15)

Harwood Childs was a man of integrity—a teacher, a scholar, a writer, an authority in his field of public opinion, a leader in his church, a devoted husband, father, grandfather, brother, friend—whose life was a beautiful balance of the old and the new, the traditional and the contemporary, the intellectual and the practical. He blended intelligence with tact, knowledge with wisdom, ability with humility, conviction with compassion, concern with good humor.

We who knew him are grateful for these qualities, and for his cheerful disposition, for as the writer of Proverbs says, "A cheerful heart is a good medicine" (Prov. 17:22).

No wonder children loved him so. He understood them; he related to them; he enjoyed them; he was like one of them.

And calling to him a child, Jesus put him in the midst of them, and said, "Truly, I say to you, unless you turn and become like children, you will never enter the kingdom of heaven. Whoever humbles himself like this child, he is the greatest in the kingdom of heaven.

"Whoever receives one such child in my name receives me."
(Matthew 18:2–5)

See that you do not despise one of these little ones; for I tell
you that in heaven their angels always behold the face of my
Father who is in heaven. . . . So it is not the will of my Father
who is in heaven that one of these little ones should perish.
(Matthew 18:10–11, 14)

How grateful, then, we should be for what these two lives have
meant to all of us. How grateful for their faith, knowing that with
Paul they too could say, "I have fought the good fight, I have
finished the race, I have kept the faith. Henceforth there is laid up
for me the crown of righteousness, which the Lord, the righteous
judge, will award to me on that Day, and not only to me but also
to all who have loved his appearing" (2 Tim. 4:7–8).

How grateful for their faith, how grateful for their love, a love
which came close to matching Paul's exquisite description of
Christian love in his letter to the Corinthians:

If I speak in the tongues of men and of angels, but have not
love, I am a noisy gong or a clanging cymbal. And if I have
prophetic powers, and understand all mysteries and all knowledge, and if I have all faith, so as to remove mountains, but
have not love, I am nothing. If I give away all I have, and if I
deliver my body to be burned, but have not love, I gain nothing.

Love is patient and kind; love is not jealous or boastful; it is
not arrogant or rude. Love does not insist on its own way; it
is not irritable or resentful; it does not rejoice at wrong, but
rejoices in the right. Love bears all things, believes all things,
hopes all things, endures all things.

Love never ends; as for prophecies, they will pass away; as
for tongues, they will cease; as for knowledge, it will pass
away. For our knowledge is imperfect and our prophecy is
imperfect; but when the perfect comes, the imperfect will pass
away. When I was a child, I spoke like a child, I thought like
a child, I reasoned like a child; when I became a man, I gave
up childish ways. For now we see in a mirror dimly, but then
face to face. Now I know in part; then I shall understand fully,
even as I have been fully understood. So faith, hope, love
abide, these three; but the greatest of these is love.

(1 Corinthians 13)

We shared the joy of their faith and love when the family gathered just a month ago for the Fiftieth Anniversary celebration of this wonderful couple. It was a happy occasion, as we reminisced and laughed together. But we sensed, too, the depth of their faith and love, so beautifully expressed in the words of Robert Browning, which were never more movingly quoted than they were that day by a loving wife to her husband of half a century:

> Grow old along with me!
> The best is yet to be,
> The last of life, for which the first was made:
> Our times are in his hand
> Who saith, "A whole I planned,
> Youth shows but half; trust God: see all, nor be afraid!"[53]

Surely the Lord has said to Willa and Harwood Childs, "Well done, thou good and faithful servant: thou hast been faithful over a few things, I will make thee ruler over many things: enter thou into the joy of thy Lord" (Matt. 25:21, KJV).

Let their death, therefore, teach us to celebrate life. And let it be a cause, not for despair, but for faith and hope and love. Let our sorrow be softened by our gratitude, so that we can be persuaded with Paul that "in everything God works for good with those who love him, who are called according to his purpose" (Rom. 8:28), and that "neither death, nor life, nor angels, nor principalities, nor things present, nor things to come, nor powers, nor height, nor depth, nor anything else in all creation, will be able to separate us from the love of God in Christ Jesus our Lord" (Rom. 8:38–39).

"For since we believe that Jesus died and rose again, even so, through Jesus, God will bring with him those who have fallen asleep" (1 Thess. 4:14). Let those who believe in the resurrection to eternal life, therefore, with Paul, "Rejoice in the Lord always; again I will say, Rejoice. Let all know your forbearance. The Lord is at hand. Have no anxiety about anything, but in everything by prayer and supplication with thanksgiving let your requests be made known to God. And the peace of God, which passes all understanding, will keep your hearts and your minds in Christ Jesus" (Phil. 4:4–7).

Amen.

Appendix D
Scriptural Reflections
(Armstrong Memorial Service)

The circumstances of my brother's death were quite different from those of my parents-in-law. Whereas their lives were snuffed out suddenly and tragically in a terrible highway accident, Herb died of cancer in a London, England, hospital. Whereas Dr. and Mrs. Childs were both believing Christians and active members of a church, my brother professed to be an agnostic most of his life.

I flew to London to visit Herb in the hospital as soon as I learned that his illness was terminal and his death imminent. His memorial service was held in the chapel of the school he had attended as a boy, and where he had spent a brief period as a member of the faculty. Some of his former teachers and colleagues were in the congregation that stormy morning in January of 1979. So was Dad, who was heartbroken by the loss of his son.

To provide a contrast to the scriptural reflections given at the memorial service for my wife's parents, here are excerpts of what I said at my brother's service. Instead of spelling out the passages that I read, I have simply cited the scripture references.

My father and I have shared many things across the years. We have something else in common now: each of us has lost a son.[54]

We are here, however, not to mourn Herb's death but to celebrate his life, not to list what he did but to learn who he was, and to consider his life and death from the perspective of our own faith. . . .

Herb died at the age of fifty-nine. He was a physical health buff for the last thirty of those years, with a highly disciplined program of body building and exercise. The day he went into the hospital he did his customary 140 push-ups, but they were no defense against the disease he didn't know he had. Herb's untimely death should remind us all that life is a gift, which we can never take for granted.

[Psalm 39:4–5]

We wonder why life must end for one who had so much to give, so much for which to live. Who can explain the grim irony of unfulfilled dreams and hopes denied by the stern reality of a death that comes too soon?

[1 Thessalonians 5:2–3]

But Paul didn't end on a negative note, and neither should we:

[1 Thessalonians 5:4–5, 8–9]

Herb loved his work, and he worked hard. He was one of those fortunate people who did not just work to live but who lived to work. He was indefatigable in pursuing his goals, yet he enjoyed life, and he lived it with zest and zeal. He understood what the writer of Ecclesiastes meant when he wrote:

[Ecclesiastes 3:10, 12–13]

Those whose work is all-important to them should listen as well to these words of the psalmist:

[Psalm 127:1–2]

"Therefore," said Jesus,

[Matthew 6:25–33]

Herb laughed at life. . . . He was an intriguing personality, a clever conversationalist, whose sense of humor was appreciated and whose genius was recognized by all who knew him. Some are astute observers of life's passing parade, and others are clever commentators. Herb was both. His was an amazing mind, creative as well as encyclopedic, inventive as well as analytical, practical as well as philosophical, logical as well as inquisitive.

It is understandable that such a mind would question the dogmatic claims of religion. "An honest man can never surrender an honest doubt," wrote Walter Malone in *The Agnostic's Creed.* Indeed, "to believe with certainty one must begin by doubting."[55] "If a man will begin with certainties," said Francis Bacon, "he shall end in doubts; but if he will be content to begin with doubts, he shall end in certainties."[56]

[Proverbs 3:13–14; 9:10]

I asked Herb if he believed in God, and he replied, "Dick, they say there are no atheists in foxholes. Well, I'm in a foxhole."

[Psalm 56:3–4]

As I was leaving the hospital at the end of my first day in London, I said, "Would you like me to offer a prayer, Herb?" After a moment's hesitation, he replied, "If you want to." I wasn't sure if he was simply humoring me. "I do if you want me to," I responded, and he nodded his assent. When we finished the prayer, there were tears in his eyes. . . .

The next night, as I was about to leave, Herb *asked* me to pray. As I took his hand, I questioned him again about his belief in God, and I'll never forget his reply. "I want to believe, Dick," he said, "but I don't have the same compelling evidence you have, to make me feel it is necessary to believe."

Herb respected my faith. He was a reverent agnostic. His was the honest doubt of a seeker, not the arrogant, cynical disbelief of a skeptic. It was like the doubt of Thomas, who wanted to be convinced, or that of the distraught father who cried out to Jesus, "Lord, I believe; help my unbelief," not the doubt of an H. L. Mencken, who said, "The liberation of the human mind has been best furthered by fellows who have heaved dead cats into sanctuaries and then went roistering down the highways of the world, proving to all men that doubt, after all, was safe—that the god in the sanctuary was a fraud."[57] "Faith," said Mencken, "may be defined briefly as an illogical belief in the occurrence of the improbable."[58]

That was not Herb. He wanted to be convinced. He had the intellectual honesty to ask the hard questions, because he wanted to believe, if he could believe, with integrity. We can be grateful for people like Herb, who question our easy assumptions. They keep us believers honest. Tennyson was right when he wrote in his famous poem "In Memoriam," "There lives more faith in honest doubt, believe me, than in half the creeds."[59] The words of one of the prelude selections played at the start of this service are also from Tennyson's "In Memoriam":

> Strong Son of God, immortal Love,
>   Whom we, that have not seen thy face,
>   By faith, and faith alone, embrace,
> Believing where we cannot prove.

> We have but faith: we cannot know,
> For knowledge is of things we see;
> And yet we trust it comes from thee,
> A beam in darkness: let it grow.[60]

Charlotte Elliott speaks for us all in a hymn whose powerful message is sometimes forgotten because of its association with evangelistic altar calls:

> Just as I am, though tossed about
> With many a conflict, many a doubt,
> Fightings and fears within, without,
> O Lamb of God, I come, I come!

. . . It's hard for a person like Herb to have faith, when there is so much evil and suffering in the world. Where is the joy of believing, when tragedy strikes?

[1 Peter 1:6–9]
[2 Corinthians 4:7–9, 16–18]

If there is no life after death, then there is no meaning to life before death. But if there is life beyond the grave, then one can live with hope, knowing that life has a purpose and the future has meaning, for life is a gift of God and the future is in God's hands. So Paul could write to the Roman Christians:

[Romans 8:18, 28, 31–35, 37–39]

That kind of confidence comes only through faith in God. A nonbeliever can die with courage; only a believer can die with confidence. Courage is an effort of the will; peace is a product of faith. Herb was a man of tremendous courage. His doctor told me he had never known a braver man. Herb had an incredible will to live. What I was trying to help him discover was the secret of Christian contentment, so that he could say with the apostle Paul:

[Philippians 4:12–13]

The person who has that kind of faith not only can live with courage but also can die with confidence. Those who know Jesus Christ and the power of his resurrection need not fear death. What all of us should want for a dying loved one is not the denial but the acceptance of death, so that he or she can die in peace. As a pastor, the more I see of death and dying, the more convinced I become of the necessity for honesty among the members of a family facing the crisis of a terminal illness. When there is a limited time available, loved ones want and need to say many things to each other, and to get their affairs in order, not to mention making their peace with God.

There is one more thing I want to say about Herb. Although our relationship as brothers had existed over half a century, our friendship had grown steadily in recent years, thanks to his frequent visits to the States, my occasional trips to England, and a steady correspondence in between. It was not until my time with Herb in the hospital, however, that I realized how great was his capacity for love. How proud he was of his two bright sons, Mark and Paul, who were the apple of his eye. His illness only deepened his appreciation and affection for them, and for his lovely wife, Emilia, who was by his bedside morning, noon, and night throughout his hospitalization. . . .

Herb loved his family in London and his family in America, and I can personally testify that he was a loving father and husband, a proud son, a loyal brother, and a most generous uncle. We can be grateful to God for Herb's remarkable talents, his keen intellect, and for his professional skills. We who loved him shall miss him, but we need not despair, for love is stronger than death.

[1 John 4:7–8, 12]

Amen.

Appendix E
Preaching Plan

The sample preaching plan or sermon schedule on the following pages covers part of a year. The format can be expanded to include the hours of worship, when there are two or more services; the initials of the preachers and liturgists sharing these responsibilities; and a column for comments. The hymns are all from The Hymnbook, *jointly published in 1955 by the Presbyterian Church in the United States, The United Presbyterian Church in the U.S.A., and the Reformed Church in America.*

Date	Special Services	Sermon Title
1/6	Ord./Inst. Serv.	"A Mind to Work"
1/13	Baptism	"News Time"
1/20	Seminary Sun.	"The Making of a Minister"
1/27		"The Spot on the Wall"
2/3	Communion Sun.	"The Cup of Demons"
2/10	Recept. New Membs.	"Not on These Rocks!"
2/17		"Jesus and Justice"
2/20	Ash Wed. Com.	"True Confessions"
2/24	1st Sun. in Lent Com.	"Christ and the Issues of Today" 1. "Christ and Liberation"
3/3	2d Sun. in Lent Baptism	2. "Christ and the Economy"
3/10	3d Sun. in Lent	3. "Christ and the Energy Crisis"
3/17	4th Sun. in Lent	4. "Christ and the Arms Race"

S-No.	Text	Scripture Passages	Hymns
734	Neh. 4:6	Neh. 4:1–6 1 Cor. 3:10–15	174, 176, 297
735	Luke 8:1	Isa. 52:1–10 Luke 8:1–8	498, 184, 383
736	Rom. 10:14	Jer. 1:4–10 Rom. 10:5–17	1, 306, 295
737	1 Cor. 10:13	Resp. Read., Sel. 17 1 Cor. 10:1–13	24, 394, 362
738	1 Cor. 10:21	Resp. Read., Sel. 5 1 Cor. 10:14–21	4, 442, 445
739	Heb. 6:4–6	Hos. 11:1–7 2 Peter 2:17–22; Heb. 6:1–8	132, 437, 350
740	Luke 11:42	Isa. 42:1–7 Luke 6:1–11; 11:42–44	110, 416, 480
741	1 John 1:9	Resp. Read., Sel. 8 1 John 1:5–10	200, 278, 445
742	Luke 4:18	Isa. 35:1–6 Luke 4:14–21	85, 235, 513
743	Luke 16:13	Deut. 8:11–20 Luke 16:1–13	358, 228, 481
744	Luke 19:26	Isa. 24:1–6 Luke 19:11–27	96, 108, 101
745	Luke 21:10	Ps. 33:12–22 Luke 21:10–19	487, 490, 483

Appendix F
A Tomb

The following sermon was part of a Lenten series entitled "Landmarks in the Life of Christ." The landmarks and texts, all from the Gospel of Mark, were as follows:

"A River" (Mark 1:1–11)   "A Cross" (Mark 15:21–39)

"A Desert" (Mark 1:12–13)   "A Road" (Mark 11:1–10)

"A Mountain" (Mark 9:2–9)   "A Garden" (Mark 14:32–50)

"A Palace" (Mark 15:1–20)   "A Tomb" (Mark 15:42–16:8)

The final sermon in the series was preached on Easter. I chose this particular way to share my own belief in the resurrection. Because the sermon was my response to an imaginary individual, I had to place the other "character" as if there were just the two of us, facing each other and alone. Therefore, there was no eye contact with the congregation throughout the entire sermon. It is impossible to recapture in print the impact of my body language, face language, and delivery, which were crucial to conveying a conversational style. The "reactions" of the Professor had to be surmised from my expressions, intonations, and gestures, as well as from the words. The person to whom I was speaking was obviously an intellectual agnostic, who, having given me all the reasons for not believing, was curious to know why I believe in the resurrection.

I have listened to you with great interest, Professor, and now I'd like to respond, if you will allow me. First let me see if I can summarize your point of view. You are willing to admit that there was an "itinerant rabbi," as you called him, named Jesus; that he offended the Jewish authorities; that he was arrested; and that he was tried under Pontius Pilate, sentenced to death, and executed.

Beyond that you say there is not much more we can know about him
for sure. You think that most of what has been written about him
in the New Testament is legendary, and that the virgin birth and the
so-called miracles he performed were later attempts of the writers
to prove his divinity.

By the same token, you have denied the resurrection, and you
look upon the story of the empty tomb as another elaborate but
impossible attempt on the part of the disciples to prove a point. So,
too, you have said that all the details of the passion story were later
efforts by the writers to show how the Old Testament prophecies
were fulfilled by Jesus, and hence to prove that he was the Messiah.
For you, the divinity of Christ is a pagan superstition, the Christian
gospel totally irrelevant, and the resurrection a meaningless myth.
I realize that you said much more, but is that a fair summary?

Okay. Let me admit from the start that neither I nor anyone else
can prove the divinity of Jesus. If I could, then you would be a
believer, right? On the other hand, neither can you disprove it; if
you could, I'd be a nonbeliever! I choose to believe, you choose not
to believe, but let us both be honest and admit that each of us brings
his own assumptions to this discussion, whether they be affirmations of faith or nonbelief.

I'm glad you agree, because I find that many nonbelievers are
unwilling to admit that their point of view is just as biased as that
of believers. Nobody is truly objective, because as soon as you talk
about being objective toward Christ, you imply that he is not your
Lord and Savior, and that is a definite point of view. You are either
for him or against him; you can't be neutral. He himself said as
much.

So I admit right at the start that I'm not neutral, that I believe in
Jesus Christ. I also admit that I *want* to believe. Having said that,
I am not going to try to muster up all kinds of arguments to prove
that Jesus was the Christ. That would be futile. What I have said
is an affirmation of faith, not the conclusion of a rational proof. If
I tried to prove it by the scriptures, you could say that my belief in
the scriptures is also a matter of faith, and you'd be right.

You were also right when you said that the case for Christianity
rests on Jesus' resurrection, which you do not accept. The apostle
Paul said the same thing: "If Christ has not been raised," he said,
"then our preaching is in vain and your faith is in vain." If the story
ended on Calvary, then everything we Christians have believed all
these centuries is wrong, and the gospel is a lie. The final landmark

in the life of Christ, however, was not the cross but the empty tomb, which for me is the symbol that Christ has indeed been raised.

I'm familiar with all the arguments you have mentioned by which people have tried to deny or disprove the resurrection. You yourself said you think the disciples invented the story to justify their desire to present Jesus as the Messiah. This would mean that Christianity is founded on a deliberate fraud, and that would hardly be in keeping with the character of the apostles, as they are presented in the New Testament. It also ignores the fact that the disciples were very skeptical and slow to believe, when they heard the report of the empty tomb. There was no disposition on their part to invent the story. Had the story been contrived, they would have eliminated all the discrepancies, don't you think? If you were making up the story, would you deliberately build into it the kinds of problems we find in the Gospels, with their different accounts, often at variance with each other?

Other critics say that Jesus was not really dead but in a coma, from which he revived in the tomb; but that theory raises more questions than it answers. How did he get out of the tomb, for one thing? How do we account for his reported appearances, for another? And why wasn't he recognizable to Mary and the disciples?

Then there's the hallucination theory, which holds that the appearances of the risen Christ were merely subjective visions on the part of those who saw him. One wonders how so many persons could have had the same subjective vision. Mass hypnosis, obviously!

The most intriguing theory, which you didn't mention—but I'm sure you're familiar with it, Professor—is that of Hugh Schonfield, who sees the death of Jesus as a plot which Jesus himself planned in order to fulfill the scriptures concerning the Messiah. According to Schonfield's theory, Jesus, who sincerely believed himself to be the Messiah, enlisted the aid of one or two trusted accomplices, without telling the disciples anything about it. When he drank the vinegar on the cross, he was drugged as previously planned, in order to appear dead. He later revived in the tomb long enough to leave instructions with his accomplices, who then buried him in an unknown grave, after he finally succumbed to his wounds. The young man mentioned in Mark's Gospel as being seen at the tomb was really one of the accomplices. Schonfield goes on to explain away the resurrection appearances in much the same manner. I keep being accosted by people who use his book, *The Passover Plot,* as their authority for disproving the resurrection.

Yes, I'm familiar with all these arguments and some others that have been advanced by skeptical scholars who feel that the story of the empty tomb and the other events described in the New Testament are the product of primitive minds and totally incompatible with modern scientific thinking. They overlook the fact, however, that some of the greatest expressions of faith in every age have come from men and women of science. Wouldn't you agree, Professor, that faith and science are not necessarily incompatible? If they were, then no doctor, or engineer, or chemist, or biologist, or a person in any other scientific or academic discipline could ever believe in Christ. But many do, including some of your own colleagues at the university.

So your conclusion regarding the resurrection is not any more inevitable than mine. The correctness of your argument is not self-evident. If it were, then I'd be forced to agree with your conclusion. But, as you well know, I don't. *However,* my reason for believing in the resurrection is not what you think it is. It does not depend on my ability to prove the fact of the empty tomb. I've already admitted that I can't prove it!

I don't know how to say what I want to say without using the kind of language which perhaps doesn't communicate to a nonbeliever, but I hope you'll listen to me, as I listened to you, and try to understand, as I attempt to say something that is really hard to get across to someone who doesn't share my assumptions. I'm not asking you to agree with me but to *understand* me.

To put it as simply as I know how, I believe in the resurrection because I have met the risen Christ.

What do I mean? I mean that I have a sense of the presence of Christ in my life. The only way I can explain it is to relate how I came to this belief, because I couldn't always say what I just said to you. Oh, I have believed in God ever since I can remember. When I was just a tiny tot, my mother taught me to say my prayers at night. I was confirmed at the age of eleven in St. Thomas Episcopal Church, in Garrison, Maryland, and my mother took me to church every Sunday. When I went away to college I attended chapel—it was compulsory in those days!—and while I was in the Navy I went to church whenever I could. I attended the services on board ship. I remember having some wonderful talks with the chaplain, and I enjoyed his sermons.

After I got married and was working, my wife and I would usually attend a church near where we were living, but we never joined, and consequently we were never really active. Even though I did believe in God and I did attend church, I never considered myself a religious person. So you can imagine my bewilderment and surprise when I suddenly felt called into the ministry.

You're smiling—how do you think I felt? We had three children at the time, and I couldn't understand why God would call me. I was the least likely candidate for the ministry, but I knew this was something I *had* to do. From that point on, I felt God was leading me, as the doors opened and closed in the most remarkable ways, until I found myself studying at Princeton Seminary.

It was there that I was confronted in a new way, and in a sense for the first time, with the person of Jesus Christ. I'm sure I had heard the words many times, but I had never got the message. I'm sure the ministers I had listened to all my life had been preaching about Christ, I just hadn't heard them. Now as I began to study the Bible and the various subjects I was taking at seminary, I realized that I had to make a decision about Christ. Could I really believe that he was the Son of God? Could I really accept him as my personal Lord and Savior? Frankly, I wasn't sure I could, and yet I knew that I must, if I expected to become a minister, or even go on calling myself a Christian.

I knew in my heart that God had called me into the ministry. I've never been more sure of anything in my faith experience. Oh, I didn't hear a voice or see a vision, or anything like that, but I knew that it was of God. It was not what my more evangelical friends described as a Christ-centered call. I believed in God, but who was Jesus?

Every day I prayed that God would give me the faith to believe in Jesus. I don't know when it happened, or how it happened, but sometime between then and now that prayer has been answered. Now I can say with the apostle Paul, for me "to live is Christ." Now I realize that what I thought was my struggle all along was really only my delayed response to what God was yearning to give me, and not only me but everyone, for his gift is offered to anyone who wants it, who is grasping for it. When God's gift and our grasp meet, that's faith!

That doesn't mean I no longer have doubts—or that faith is no longer a struggle. The Christian life is an ongoing wrestling match. Yet somehow I find myself able to say, "I believe!" I wake up believing, and I thank God for giving me the gift of faith. I can't make myself believe, and I can't possibly make anyone else believe. For it is only through and by the power of the Spirit of God that one is able to say, "I believe."

I understand that now. I didn't then. Now I realize that what happened to me is exactly what Jesus said would happen to a person: the Holy Spirit bears witness to Jesus. That is, the Spirit testifies in the heart of the believer that Christ is who he said he was. "He will take what is mine and declare it to you." The Spirit enables the believer to see that he who has seen Christ has seen the Father, that he and the Father are one, and that no one can really know God as his or her heavenly Father except through Jesus Christ. It's this indispensability that enables Christians to speak about Christ the way they do, as their personal Lord and Savior, a present, vital, dynamic reality in their lives.

That's what I mean when I say I've met the risen Christ. That's why I believe in the resurrection. Having said that, I can accept the biblical testimony. I don't need someone to prove to me the fact of the empty tomb. I don't worry about the discrepancies in the different Gospel accounts, and it doesn't bother me that we'll never know what actually happened. All I know is that *something* happened back there, because Christ is alive today. He is risen! And because he is, life has meaning, history has purpose, and there is hope for the future.

Does this make sense, Professor?

I see. But instead of trying to explain it away, why not ask yourself what happened to the disciples? How do you account for the amazing transformation in their lives? And what about the millions and millions of women and men in every age whose lives have born witness to the presence and the power of the risen Christ? I have known too many people who have felt the transforming power of the Holy Spirit, not to believe in the reality of the resurrection.

There is power in the gospel of Jesus Christ, Professor—power for living! Let me put it to you squarely: Where is the power in your philosophy? Where's the joy? Where's the hope? What good news do you have to share with the world? Does it inspire you to sing?

By the way, tomorrow is Easter. Why don't you come to church? You'll hear a lot of people who *do* have something to sing about.

And maybe you will too!

Appendix G
"Who He?"

The following sermon was preached on Pentecost. It was part of a series of sermons on the meaning of faith.

And he said to them, "Did you receive the Holy Spirit when you believed?" And they said, "No, we have never even heard that there is a Holy Spirit" (Acts 19:2).

When the apostle Paul asked the group of disciples at Ephesus if they had received the Holy Spirit, they replied, "No, we have never even heard that there is a Holy Spirit."

My experiences with new members classes, inquirers groups, and Bible study groups have convinced me that there are many people, including not a few church members, who can identify with those twelve Ephesians. They know about God and about Jesus. But the Holy Spirit—who he?

We Presbyterians cannot say we have never heard there is a Holy Spirit. There are references to the Holy Spirit (or Holy Ghost) throughout our liturgy. Every time we sing the Doxology or the Gloria Patri, the Holy Spirit is mentioned. Every time we hear a Trinitarian benediction, or see someone ordained, or confirmed, or baptized, we are reminded that there is a Holy Spirit. We have sung many, many hymns, including the three we are singing this morning, about the Holy Spirit. But I'm not sure most people understand who he is.

It's not surprising, for we are dealing with a mystery. I think it's fair to say that most Christians would be hard-pressed to explain the doctrine of the Trinity. We can talk about God, we can talk about Jesus, but the Holy Spirit—who he?

To ask "Who he?" or "Who she?" is better than asking "Who it?" for the Holy Spirit is personal. That's one of the main differences in the way the term is used in the New Testament, as compared with the Old Testament, where the Spirit of God is an "it," not a "he" or a "she." The term "Holy Spirit" occurs only three times in the Old Testament, never in the New Testament sense, in which the Holy Spirit is uniquely related to Jesus Christ. Let me quote a few verses from the Gospel of John in order to give you a feeling of that relationship. Jesus is talking to his disciples, and he tells them:

> I will pray the Father, and he will give you another Counselor, to be with you for ever, even the Spirit of truth, whom the world cannot receive, because it neither sees him nor knows him; you know him, for he dwells with you, and will be in you (John 14:16–17).

> I will not leave you desolate; I will come to you. . . . If [you] love me, [you] will keep my word, and my Father will love [you], and we will come to [you] and make our home with [you] (John 14:18, 23).

> These things I have spoken to you, while I am still with you. But the Counselor, the Holy Spirit, whom the Father will send in my name, he will teach you all things, and bring to your remembrance all that I have said to you (John 14:25–26).

> When the Counselor comes, whom I shall send to you from the Father, even the Spirit of truth, who proceeds from the Father, he will bear witness to me (John 15:26).

> Now I am going to him who sent me. . . . It is to your advantage that I go away, for if I do not go away, the Counselor will not come to you; but if I go, I will send him to you. And when he comes, he will convince the world concerning sin and righteousness and judgment (John 16:5, 7–8).

> When the Spirit of truth comes, he will guide you into all the truth. . . . He will glorify me, for he will take what is mine and declare it to you (John 16:13–14).

> I came from the Father and have come into the world; again, I am leaving the world and going to the Father (John 16:28).

Even though the word "Trinity" is not used in the New Testament, it is easy to see from such passages as these why the early church was led to spell out the doctrine of the Trinity, to clarify the relationship between the Father, the Son, and the Holy Spirit.

Note the interchangeability of the three Persons of the Trinity. In one place Jesus says, "I will not leave you desolate; I will come to you," while a little later he says, "We will come," referring to himself and the Father. In other places it is the Counselor, the Holy Spirit, who is coming, all of which verses underscore the unity amid the diversity of the Godhead, as we affirmed in our opening hymn, "God in three Persons, blessed Trinity."

Note, too, that the coming of the Holy Spirit is contingent upon the completion of Jesus' earthly ministry, "for if I do not go away, the Counselor will not come to you." The Spirit's function is to bear witness to Christ. "He will glorify me," said Jesus, "for he will take what is mine and declare it to you." The Holy Spirit is not the bearer of a new revelation, but rather the interpreter of the truth which has already been revealed in Christ. "He will teach you all things, and bring to your remembrance all that I have said to you." The world cannot receive him, "because it neither sees him nor knows him; you know him," said Jesus, "for he dwells with you, and will be in you."

Today is Pentecost, the fiftieth day counting from Easter. It is the day on which we celebrate the gift of the Holy Spirit, for it was on Pentecost that Jesus' promise was fulfilled. On that day the apostles were empowered by the Holy Spirit to go forth in the name of Christ and bear witness to their living Lord.

So also, today, it is the Holy Spirit who bears witness to Jesus Christ. The Spirit testifies in the hearts of believers that Jesus is Lord and brings them into a living relationship with him and with each other in the community of faith, which is the church. It is the Holy Spirit who reminds us that Christian faith is personal, not private; social, not individualistic.

Paul asked the Ephesians if they had received the Holy Spirit when they believed. You and I might be wondering the same thing about ourselves. Have we received the Holy Spirit? Let me suggest three rules by which you can determine an answer to that question. The first rule is *obey and receive*. When Peter and the apostles appeared before the Sanhedrin, the Jewish council, they concluded their testimony by declaring, "We are witnesses to these things, and so is the Holy Spirit whom God has given to those who obey him" (Acts 5:32).

That is a fantastic thought. God gives his Spirit *to those who obey him*. This implies that we ought to obey God whether we believe in God or not. God's moral laws are plain enough for any sincere seeker of truth to see. It's not a matter of our having to be convinced there's a God before we start obeying the moral laws which our consciences can discern. We have to act *as if* there is a God, simply because what God represents is so obviously good and true to anyone who is sincerely seeking the truth. The promise is that those who do will receive the Holy Spirit. The way to God is the path of obedience.

It's the same with prayer: the only convincing argument for prayer is praying. Similarly, the only way to know God is to do God's will. Those who obey God will receive the gift of the Holy Spirit.

Obey and receive, that's the first rule, and the second is *receive and believe*. There are passages which suggest that it is the other way around, as when Paul asked the Ephesians if they had received the Holy Spirit when they believed. Here I think Paul had in mind some manifestation of the Spirit, such as occurred at Pentecost, when the people spoke in tongues, *after* receiving the Holy Spirit. Again, we are told that when Paul had laid his hands upon the disciples at Ephesus, "the Holy Spirit came on them; and they spoke with tongues and prophesied" (Acts 19:6).

On the other hand, in his first letter to Corinth, Paul declares, "No one can say 'Jesus is Lord' except by the Holy Spirit" (1 Cor. 12:3), and to the Romans he writes, "Any one who does not have the Spirit of Christ does not belong to him" (Rom. 8:9). "By this we know that he abides in us, by the Spirit which he has given us," writes John (1 John 3:24). If, then, it is the Holy Spirit who bears witness to Christ, the Spirit must be in us in order for us to believe in Christ.

In other words, receive and believe. That makes sense to me, because that's the way it happened. I believed in God long before I understood what it meant to have a personal relationship with Jesus Christ. Now I know that Christianity *is* Jesus Christ. Apart from Christ, Christianity is just another religion. One religion is about as good as another. The uniqueness of Christianity is Christ. He is the central fact of our faith. Now I know that Christ is all in all, and that, my friends, is the work of the Holy Spirit. Once you are able to accept Jesus Christ as your personal Lord and Savior, you know it is the work of the Holy Spirit in you, bearing witness to and glorifying Christ, doing just what Jesus said the Spirit would do.

Obey and receive, receive and believe, and lastly, *believe and obey*. "Whoever believes in the Son has eternal life," writes John; "whoever does not obey the Son shall not see life, but the wrath of God rests upon that person" (John 3:36). "If you love me, you will keep my commandments," said Jesus (John 14:15). "If you keep my commandments, you will abide in my love. . . . This is my commandment, that you love one another as I have loved you" (John 15:10, 12). Obedience is the fruit and the proof of faith. If we say we believe in Christ and don't obey God, we make liars of ourselves, and we call into question our discipleship. Just as it is the Holy Spirit who empowers us to believe, so it is the Holy Spirit who empowers us to obey. He inspires every noble deed, every worthy desire, every impulse for good.

So we have come full circle. If we believe, we obey, and when we obey we receive. But our obedience must find its direction in relation to Christ, in whom we believe, as Paul says, taking "every thought captive to obey Christ" (2 Cor. 10:5). As the Spirit teaches us all things, and brings to our remembrance and understanding the things Jesus said, we begin to see what Jesus meant when he said such things as, "I am the way, and the truth, and the life; no one comes to the Father, but by me" (John 14:6). "I and the Father are one" (John 10:30). "Whoever has seen me has seen the Father" (John 14:9). "I am the resurrection and the life" (John 11:25). "I am the living bread which came down from heaven" (John 6:51). "I am the light of the world" (John 8:12).

That is why Christians can talk about a personal relationship with Christ, who calls us to be his witnesses to the uttermost parts of the earth, and who promises to be with us always, to the end of time. It is not that Jesus becomes a substitute for God, as a Jewish friend of mine charged recently. It is that God's nature and God's purpose for humankind have been revealed in Jesus. As the writer of Hebrews puts it, "He reflects the glory of God and bears the very stamp of his nature" (Heb. 1:3). When we finally come to understand that, we realize it is the work of the Holy Spirit, doing exactly what Jesus said he would do—bearing witness to him.

So:
> Obey God and receive the Holy Spirit;
> receive the Holy Spirit and believe in Jesus Christ;
> believe in Christ and obey God.

Let us pray:
> Spirit of God, descend upon my heart;
>   Wean it from earth; through all its pulses move;
> Stoop to my weakness, mighty as thou art,
>   And make me love thee as I ought to love. Amen.

Notes

1. Charles L. Goodell, *Pastor and Evangelist* (George H. Doran Co., 1922), pp. 19–20. The title of the first chapter is "The Pastor-Evangelist." Of all the references consulted, Goodell's two books, *Pastor and Evangelist* and *Pastoral and Personal Evangelism,* come closest to addressing some aspects of the general theme that is explored in my book *The Pastor as Evangelist* (Westminster Press, 1984) and this present book.

2. Robert Menzies, *Preaching and Pastoral Evangelism* (Saint Andrew Press, 1963), pp. 10–11. The language is dated but the ideas are not.

3. Frank C. Senn, *The Pastor as Worship Leader: A Manual for Corporate Worship* (Augsburg Publishing House, 1977), p. 95. This is a brief but thorough study of the theology and practice of worship from a Lutheran perspective. It is not evangelistically concerned, except for one reference to the ushers' alerting the pastor regarding visitors in worship (p. 108).

4. Donald Macleod, *Presbyterian Worship: Its Meaning and Method,* rev. ed. (John Knox Press, 1980), ch. 2. A very practical book on worship in the Reformed tradition, with helpful insights from the author's experience as a Presbyterian minister and professor of homiletics. Some other useful books on worship are *Faithful and Fair* (Abingdon Press, 1981), by Keith Watkins, who makes a reasonable case for the use of inclusive language in worship; *Worship as Pastoral Care* (Abingdon Press, 1979), by William H. Willimon; and *Introduction to Christian Worship* (Abingdon Press, 1980), by James F. White.

5. *The Constitution of the Presbyterian Church (U.S.A.),* Part II: *Book of Order,* S-2.0400.

6. James S. Stewart, *Heralds of God* (Charles Scribner's Sons,

1946), p. 72. This is one of the classic books on preaching, covering the preacher's world, theme, study, technique, and inner life.

7. Gerard S. Sloyan makes the same point in his book *Worshipful Preaching* (Fortress Press, 1984): "Preachers are leaders in prayer. Our preaching is one of the several prayerful things we do in a context of worship. More accurately, preaching is part of the one, prayerful thing we do publicly. This being so, the homily must above all be an integral part of the worship service" (pp. 11–12). Norman Pittenger likewise has examined the task of preaching in a liturgical context in his book *Preaching the Gospel* (Morehouse-Barlow Co., 1984). See especially the chapter entitled "The Setting in Worship."

8. Donald P. Ellsworth's book *Christian Music in Contemporary Witness* (Baker Book House, 1980) is a useful aid to thinking evangelistically about church music. See also Albert Edward Bailey's classic work, *The Gospel in Hymns* (Charles Scribner's Sons, 1954); Erik Routley's *Church Music and the Christian Faith* (Agape, 1978); and Eileen Southern's *The Music of Black Americans: A History* (W. W. Norton & Co., 1971).

9. Jessica Mitford, *The American Way of Death* (Simon & Schuster, 1963), ch. 6.

10. Andrew W. Blackwood's book *The Funeral* (Westminster Press, 1942) is still an excellent resource.

11. George E. Sweazey, *Preaching the Good News* (Prentice-Hall, 1976), p. 235. This is a complete textbook on preaching and a practical resource for every pastor's personal library.

12. *The Passion for Souls* was the title of one of John Henry Jowett's books.

13. Goodell, *Pastor and Evangelist*, p. 37.

14. Goodell, *Pastoral and Personal Evangelism*, p. 115. Though somewhat dated, much of the content is still relevant, including a chapter on "Evangelistic Preaching."

15. Menzies, *Preaching and Pastoral Evangelism*, p. 108.

16. John Henry Jowett, *The Preacher, His Life and Work* (George H. Doran Co., 1912), p. 24. These Yale Lectures delivered by the famous former pastor of the Fifth Avenue Presbyterian Church of New York City are as powerful, inspiring, and pertinent as when they were first published.

17. Ibid., p. 171.

18. W. E. Sangster, *Power in Preaching* (Abingdon Press, 1958), p. 19. This is a clearly written, well-organized little book by a

British Methodist preacher and author, containing his Fondren Lectures, delivered at Southern Methodist University in Dallas, Texas.

19. George A. Buttrick, *Jesus Came Preaching* (Charles Scribner's Sons, 1932), p. 181.

20. Halford E. Luccock, *Communicating the Gospel* (Harper & Brothers, 1954), p.43.

21. Quoted by Goodell in *Pastoral and Personal Evangelism*, p. 54.

22. Andrew W. Blackwood, *Planning a Year's Pulpit Work* (Abingdon-Cokesbury Press, 1942), p. 15.

23. For those who may be looking for ideas, there are many resources, such as David A. MacLennan's book *Resources for Sermon Preparation* (Westminster Press, 1957), which offers sermon ideas for the seasons of the Christian year and other special Sundays on the church calendar. "Every Christian preacher has inexhaustible resources," wrote MacLennan in the preface to the book. "Nevertheless, there comes to the most faithful transmitter of the Word arid stretches on his homiletical pilgrimage" (p. 7). For a more recent and different look at the role and importance of the gift of imagination and its relation to creativity in preaching, see Robert D. Young's *Religious Imagination* (Westminster Press, 1979).

24. Quoted by Menzies, *Preaching and Pastoral Evangelism*, p. 150.

25. Sweazey, *Preaching the Good News*, pp. 233–235.

26. J. Randall Nichols has applied the insights of communication theory to preaching in his book *Building the Word: The Dynamics of Communication and Preaching* (Harper & Row, 1981). See also Leslie J. Tizard's book, *Preaching: The Art of Communication* (Oxford University Press, 1958). Halford Luccock called this "an amazing book . . . a sheer miracle in itself," referring to the fact that it was published after the untimely death of the author, who was never able to complete the project he had started after learning of his terminal illness. The two chapters on the personality of the preacher and the chapter on the art of communication are both inspirational and practical. Donald G. Miller's book *The Way to Biblical Preaching* (Abingdon Press, 1957) addresses the topic "How to Communicate the Gospel in Depth." For a speech professor's thoughts on preaching, see Ralph L. Lewis' book *Persuasive Preaching Today* (revised, self-published edition,

1979), which focuses on the techniques rather than the content of preaching. See also Robert D. Young's book *Be Brief About It* (Westminster Press, 1980), which makes the case for shorter sermons and for using no more words than necessary to say what we have to say.

27. Menzies, *Preaching and Pastoral Evangelism*, pp. 25–27.

28. For the .views of thirteen distinguished preachers on the art of sermon construction, see *Here Is My Method*, edited by Donald Macleod (Fleming H. Revell Co., 1952). Two other helpful books that have stood the test of time are W. E. Sangster's *The Craft of the Sermon* (Epworth Press, 1954) and John A. Broadus' *On the Preparation and Delivery of Sermons*, originally published in 1870. Henry Fort Newton referred to Broadus' book, as updated and completely revised by Jesse Burton Weatherspoon (Harper & Brothers, 1944), as "the standard and classic book in the field of preacher-craft" (book jacket).

29. Armstrong, *The Pastor as Evangelist*, p. 51. Mortimer Arias has presented a thorough treatment of the kingdom of God and its importance for evangelization in his book *Announcing the Reign of God* (Fortress Press, 1984).

30. In *The Pastor as Evangelist*, I have devoted a chapter to a discussion of the meaning of evangelism, in which I have listed twenty or more definitions from a wide variety of sources. Included in the discussion is my own description of "service evangelism." The term refers to a particular style of evangelism described in my book *Service Evangelism* (see especially ch. 4). It is the evangelistic outreach of a church whose members take seriously what it means to be a community of faith and the servant people of God. For further study of the meaning of evangelism, see Douglas Webster's excellent book *What Is Evangelism?* (Highway Press, 1961); George E. Sweazey's *Effective Evangelism*, rev. ed. (Harper & Row, 1976) and his *The Church as Evangelist* (Harper & Row, 1978); Delos Miles's *Introduction to Evangelism* (Broadman Press, 1983); Ben C. Johnson's *An Evangelism Primer: Practical Principles for Congregations* (John Knox Press, 1983); Harvie M. Conn's *Evangelism: Doing Justice and Preaching Grace* (Zondervan Publishing House, 1982); and David M. Stowe's *Ecumenicity and Evangelism* (Wm. B. Eerdmans Publishing Co., 1970).

31. For an understanding of the application of narrative theology to the task of preaching, see Eugene Lowry's books *The Homile-*

tical Plot: The Sermon as Narrative Art Form (John Knox Press, 1980) and *Doing Time in the Pulpit* (Abingdon Press, 1985).

32. Gerhard Kittel and Gerhard Friedrich, eds., *Theological Dictionary of the New Testament*, Vol. 4 (Wm. B. Eerdmans Publishing Co., 1967), pp. 985–986.

33. Ibid., Vol. 3 (1966), p. 703.

34. Ibid., p. 706.

35. Ibid., pp. 710, 711, 714, 716.

36. *Theological Dictionary of the New Testament*, Vol. 2 (1965), p. 570.

37. Ian Macpherson, *The Burden of the Lord* (Abingdon Press, 1955), p. 10. Here is another perspective on the preacher and preaching from the pen of an evangelical Scottish minister.

38. My present working definition of evangelism is found in chapter 10.

39. "A Theological Reflection . . . ," p. 15.

40. The 195th General Assembly (1983) of The United Presbyterian Church U.S.A., declared that the Church's "witness to Jesus Christ, as expressed in evangelism, is a necessary, urgent, and major priority of the Church." In 1985 the 197th General Assembly approved a far-reaching plan designed to make evangelism and church membership growth a central priority of the newly formed Presbyterian Church (U.S.A.).

41. "Beth El News" (Congregation Beth El, Cherry Hill, New Jersey, March 1973), p. 3.

42. *Newsweek,* August 13, 1978, p. 45.

43. David M. Stowe, *Ecumenicity and Evangelism* (Wm. B. Eerdmans Publishing Co., 1970), p. 12.

44. Dean Kelley, *Why Conservative Churches Are Growing* (Harper & Row, 1972).

45. Donald McGavran, *Understanding Church Growth,* rev. ed. (Wm. B. Eerdmans Publishing Co., 1980), p. 223.

46. C. Peter Wagner, *Your Church Can Grow* (Regal Books, 1976), p. 110.

47. Gibson Winter, *The Suburban Captivity of the Churches* (Doubleday & Co., 1961), pp. 66–67, 69.

48. *Your Church Can Grow,* p. 158. Dr. Wagner and other representatives of the Church Growth Movement have modified their position in recent years to incorporate a greater concern for the church's social action ministry. They have also made it clear that they do not advocate a noninclusive outreach; they are simply

stressing the fact that people prefer to associate with "their own kind." As one who has been critical of the application of the so-called "homogeneous unit principle" to the ministry of evangelism, I again want to express my genuine appreciation for the tremendous help many churches have received from the diagnostic observations, programmatic ideas, and practical methods of the Church Growth Movement.

49. Stowe, *Ecumenicity and Evangelism.*

50. *The Constitution of the Presbyterian Church (U.S.A.),* Part I: *Book of Confessions,* 9.30.

51. "Seven Proofs God Exists," pamphlet published and distributed by the Radio Church of God, 1960.

52. George W. Crane, "The Worry Clinic," *Indianapolis Star,* February 23, 1977.

53. "Rabbi Ben Ezra," stanza i.

54. Our son Ricky died of leukemia at the age of five and a half.

55. Stanislaus, king of Poland, *Maxims.*

56. Francis Bacon, *The Advancement of Learning,* bk. I, v, 8.

57. H. L. Mencken, in *The American Mercury,* January 1924.

58. Mencken, in *Prejudices, Third Series,* ch. 14.

59. Alfred, Lord Tennyson, "In Memoriam," 96, st. 3.

60. Ibid., Introduction.

Index

Accompaniment, 35–36, 65; free, 36; to reading, 67
Address of church, 27, 28, 29, 174
Affirmation of faith, 19, 52, 89, 105, 116, 126, 128, 131–133, 134, 141, 192
Agnostic(s), 89, 110, 133, 185–186, 192–197
Aides: see Minister's aides
Altar call, 117, 126
Ambition, pastor's, 150
American Association of Theological Schools, 170
Anglican, 45, 162; see also Episcopalian
Announcements, 23, 35, 66, 95, 114, 125
Anthem(s), 17, 34, 37, 77, 78
Apologists, 116
Appeals for response, 67, 86, 110, 117–118, 121, 123, 125–126, 147
Area code, 29, 174
Arias, Mortimer, 206
Arrogance, 157–158, 163
Assumptions, 81, 116, 171, 193, 195
Attendance, 54, 56, 62, 64–65, 70, 74, 95, 120; boosting, 172; registration, 48, 49
Attitude(s), 30, 54, 110; toward preaching, 149–160
Authenticity, 113; see also Honesty
Authority, 88, 107, 149, 151–156; of the Bible, 129–130; for evangelism, 162; of Jesus, 152–

154; preachers', 129, 151–152, 155–156, 171; test of, 153–156
Awareness, preacher's, 16, 27, 30, 40, 161–165; of people, 110–112, 121; of self, 116; of trust, 150, 158

Bacon, Francis, 185, 208
Bailey, Albert Edward, 204
Balance, in preaching, 119–120, 165–169; see also Worship, balance in
Baptism, 50–53, 139, 141; instruction for, 50–51
Baptist churches, 45, 163
Baxter, Richard, 87
Belief(s), 127–148, 153, 185–187, 192–197, 198–202; of the church, 45, 75, 77; pastor's, 21, 61, 76, 81, 88–89, 117, 157, 163, 169–172
Bible, 26, 55, 66, 76, 91, 94, 96, 97, 101, 106–107, 121, 129–131
Blackwood, Andrew, 92, 204, 205
Body (and face) language, 37, 47, 116, 121, 192
Broadus, John A., 206
Brooks, Phillips, 90
Browning, Robert, 183
Bulletin: see Church bulletin
Burden, preacher's, 157, 159–160, 207
Buttrick, George, 87, 205

Call of God, 76, 77, 79, 87, 100, 141, 151, 152, 157, 169–170, 196

Calvin, John, 24, 46
Catholic: *see* Roman Catholic
Celebration: communion, 24, 25, 46–49, 58; life, 62; ordination, 79; special occasions, 37–39
Charge, 76, 77, 80
Choir(s), 30, 31, 37, 78
Christ: *see* Jesus Christ
Christian(s), 51, 58, 75, 127, 130, 131, 137, 164, 168, 198, 201
Christian year, 25, 31, 38, 92, 96
Christmas, 25, 26, 38, 89
Church, churches, 45–46, 50–51, 75–77, 124–125, 148, 167–169, and passim
Church bulletin, 18, 34, 78, 95, 98, 114; as evaluation instrument, 26–30, 174–177
Church Growth Movement, 167–169, 207–208
Church hopping (shopping), 77, 97, 120
Clarity, 23, 25, 46, 77, 113
Clerical garb, 43, 49, 78
Commandment(s), 139, 140, 141, 143–146, 147, 148, 202
Commission, 146–148, 149, 162, 164
Commitment, 21, 51, 76, 77, 80, 86, 87, 88, 117, 123, 133, 142, 144, 158, 169, 170
Committal service, 66, 68, 71
Communication, 16, 20, 27, 41, 65, 101, 104, 111–112, 115, 116, 117, 121, 169, 195, 205; preaching as, 150–151
Communication theory, 111, 113
Communion: *see* Holy Communion
Community, 16, 17, 38, 75, 80–81; of faith, 52, 149, 168, 170, 200
Compassion, 87
Conditional aspect of the gospel, 138–143
Congregation: and awareness, 19–20, 21, 23, 33, 34, 35, 36, 40, 57, 66, 68, 72, 75, 94, 101, 113, 114; as challenge to preacher, 110, 119; evangelistic role of, 10, 16, 40–41, 43, 79, 80, 102; and

music, 30–37, 57, 67, 69, 78; needs of, 26, 110, 119; participation of, 16, 18, 22, 23, 27, 30, 31, 32, 36, 39, 40, 57, 58, 67, 68, 79–80, 95, 111, 116, 128; response of, 91, 115, 118, 119, 121, 122, 129, 150–151
Conn, Harvie M., 206
Conscience, 101–102
Consistency, 50, 88, 115, 116
Content: church bulletin, 27, 78; sermon, 69, 102, 107–108, 109, 115, 118, 122, 123–148; worship service, 16, 17
Contentment, 98, 137–138, 187
Context, 15, 20, 52, 54, 62, 68, 72, 86, 114, 115, 125–126, 167
Conversations, 41, 55–56, 59; style of, 102, 104
Conversion, 123, 141–142
Conviction(s), 21, 33, 77, 87, 89, 157, 163
Coping, 136–138
Crane, George W., 208
Credibility, 169–172; *see also* Authenticity
Creed(s), 18, 19, 29, 126, 175, 186
Criteria: for hymn selection, 31–34; for special music, 34; for worship theme, 25–26
Criticism, 90, 129, 130

Death, 26, 61–62, 63, 64, 65, 72–73, 135–136, 142, 178–179, 187–188
Death notice, 63
Decision(s): faith, 16, 17, 22, 54, 56, 67, 85, 86, 110, 117, 118, 123, 125, 126, 132, 133, 162, 196; to join church, 16, 17, 22, 40, 70, 76, 80, 133
Delivery, sermon, 56–57, 67–68, 71, 103–105, 109–122, 149, 159, 205
Demands of the gospel, 143–148
Direction, in preaching, 118–121
Directory for the Service of God, 24–25
Discipleship, 50, 143, 146, 147, 162, 168, 202

Doubt(s), 110, 128, 171, 185–187, 196

Easter, 25, 197, 200
Eastern Orthodox churches, 45, 75
Ecumenical, 80–81, 162, 164
Elliott, Charlotte, 187
Ellsworth, Donald P., 204
Episcopalian, 45, 46; *see also* Anglican
Eucharist: *see* Holy Communion
Eulogy, 62, 68
Evangelical, 118, 123, 125
Evangelism, 10, 34, 40, 54, 59, 85–86, 88, 110; challenges to, 163–165; defined, 124–125, 145, 151, 154, 206; integrity of, 161–173; mandate for, 162–163, 164, 165
Event(s): current, 94; preaching as event, 86, 91, 111, 121–122, 149; social, 59–60; special, 26, 33, 37–38, 80
Existence of God, 171–172
Expectancy, 116–117
Explaining, 16, 18–19, 23, 30–31, 40, 55, 113, 140; *see also* Instruction; Interpretation; Teaching
Eye contact, 20, 56, 57, 104, 121
Eyewitnesses, 128–129

Facial expressions: *see* Language
Faith, 74, 128, 131, 132, 153, 186–187, 193, 195, 196; gift of, 196–197; and obedience, 200–202; the pastor's, 21, 61, 78, 80, 81, 87, 89, 91, 103, 116, 169–172; of people, 26, 51, 52, 62, 64, 85, 110, 118, 119, 120, 131
Faith sharing, 21, 55–56, 72, 80, 81, 116, 160
Farrington, Harry Webb, 131
Fees, 70
Fellowship hour, 42–43
File(s): funeral aids, 66, 71–72; illustrations, 98–99; sermon ideas, 96–97; sermons, 95, 103, 106
First-person sermons, 39, 114–115, 122, 192–197

Forgiveness, 51, 123, 134–135, 139, 142, 146, 147
Friedrich, Gerhard, 207
Friendliness, 16, 18, 40–41, 80, 115
Funeral(s), 61–73, 204

Godparents, 50–51
Goodell, Charles L., 9, 87, 203, 204, 205
Gospel (good news), 26, 39, 60, 62, 64, 66, 67, 68, 86, 88, 94, 95, 110, 114, 123–148, 162, 169; paradox, 140–141; promises of, 134–138; social, 124, 138, 145; the how, 134–138; the ifs, 138–143; the therefores, 143–148; the what, 127; the where, 125–126; the who, 131–133; the why, 127–131
Gospel song, 33
Graveside service, 70–71
Gray, Thomas, 135
Greeters, 29, 41, 175

Hankey, Katherine, 127
Holy Communion, 25, 45–50, 176; for the sick, 49; at weddings, 58
Holy Spirit, 26, 36, 60, 76, 86–87, 90–91, 97, 104–105, 116, 118, 122, 130–131, 137, 138, 139, 147, 162, 171, 172, 197, 198–202
Homogeneous unit principle, 167–168
Honesty, 62, 134, 171–172; *see also* Authenticity
Honoraria: *see* Fees
Hope, 61, 64, 67, 70, 76, 134, 136, 137, 141, 143, 197
Hymn(s), 17, 18, 19, 25, 30–34, 35, 94–95, 125; at funerals, 64–65, 66, 67, 68, 69; at ordination, 77, 78; at weddings, 57
Hymnbook, The, 32
Hymnals, 17, 18, 33

"I ams" of Jesus, the, 132–133, 202
Idea(s), 15, 24, 30, 39; sermon, 95–97

Illustrations, sermon, 25, 35, 66, 90, 93, 94, 97, 98–101, 105, 107, 112, 113, 115, 121, 127

Impression(s): of Christians, 163–164; of Jesus, 127; of ministers, 70, 89, 116, 155; of worship, 16–17, 22, 40, 42, 49

Indolence, 158

Insincerity, 157, 172

Installation service, 79–81

Instruction, 113; re baptism, 50–51; re communion, 47; re funerals, 72; re marriage, 55, 56–59

Integrity, 88–89, 91, 92, 113, 118, 133, 147; of evangelism, 161–173

Interest, 16, 18, 20, 26, 34, 37, 93, 95, 98, 115

Interpretation: of aspects of worship, 16, 18–19, 20, 23, 25, 36, 39, 46, 50; by Jesus, 130; by scribes, 152

Invitation: to commitment, 19, 117, 118, 126; to communion, 46; to ministers, 56, 74, 159; to ordination reception, 78; to "pay last respects," 69; to worship, 23, 40, 79

Jesus Christ, 9, 45, 51, 53, 54, 61, 62, 76, 81, 85, 86, 87, 88, 89, 107, 116, 123–124; authority of, 152–154; case for, 192–197; demands of, 143–148; life of, 127; love of, 167, 169; mandate from, 162; promises of, 134–138; response to, 138–143; witnesses to, 129–131

Jews, 62, 130, 163–164, 165, 168, 200

John (apostle), 128; Gospel of, 124, 135, 199, 201–202

Johnson, Ben C., 206

Joining the church, 16, 17, 28–29, 40, 56, 76, 77, 80, 133

Jowett, John Henry, 87, 204

Joy, 79, 115, 137, 143, 183, 187, 197

Justice, 134, 145, 147, 152, 167

Kelley, Dean, 167, 207

Kingdom of God (heaven), 123–124, 139, 140, 168

Kittel, Gerhard, 207

Language, 23, 33, 34, 87, 113, 165, 166, 195; evangelical, 118, 123, 125; face and body, 37, 47, 116, 121, 192

Lay participation, 159–160; *see also* Participants

Lewis, Ralph L., 205

Liberation theology, 145–146

Life: abundant, 87, 132, 136–138, 141; Christian, 86, 124, 132–133; devotional, 89–90; eternal, 61, 86, 123, 130, 132–133, 135–136, 139, 141; of Jesus, 127, 146

Linguistic analysis, 164

Listening, 16, 20, 37, 42, 47, 59, 89, 91, 111, 112, 113, 114, 115, 120, 151, 156

Liturgy, 16, 18, 22, 24, 32, 43, 46, 75, 79–80

Logical positivism, 164

Lord's Supper: *see* Holy Communion

Love, 182–183; for God, 62, 137, 139, 143; of God, 51, 62, 131, 136, 137, 138–144, 162; of others, 18, 63, 64, 115, 140, 143–147, 182–183

Lowry, Eugene, 206

Luccock, Halford, 87–88, 205

Luther, Martin, 24, 75, 113

Lutheran, 18, 45

MacLennan, David A., 205

Macleod, Donald, 24, 97, 203, 206

Macpherson, Ian, 157, 207

Malone, Walter, 185

Manuscript, sermon, 57, 90, 101–106, 121–122

Marriage, 54, 55; *see also* Weddings

Martyn, Henry, 88

McGavran, Donald, 167, 207

Member(s), church, 15, 19, 22, 25, 34, 41, 42, 43, 48, 49, 53, 65, 72, 76, 77, 79, 80, 93, 95, 98, 110, 113; prospective, 18, 123, 133

Membership, preparing for, 50, 133

Memorial services, 65, 66, 68, 70; Herbert E. Armstrong, Jr., 184–188; Harwood and Willa Childs, 178–183; *see also* Funerals
Mencken, H. L., 186, 208
Menzies, Robert, 9, 87, 117, 203, 204, 205, 206
Method, 90, 102, 103–104, 121–122
Miles, Delos, 206
Miller, Donald G., 205
Minister(s), 20, 51, 54, 56, 58, 60, 72, 76–80, 88, 89, 121, 159
Minister's aides, 42
Ministry, 11, 26, 51, 70, 74, 75, 76, 77, 79, 150, 152; evangelistic, 27, 37, 41, 60, 87, 148; of Jesus, 145–146; preaching, 92, 95, 103, 107, 119–120, 121, 151, 155, 158, 159–160
Mitford, Jessica, 65, 204
Music, 17, 18, 22–23, 30–37, 204; at communion, 48; coordinating, 94, 166; at funerals, 65, 67, 69; at ordination, 78; special music, 26, 34; transition, 36; at weddings, 57
Music director, 34, 94

Narrative theology, 101, 127
National Council of Churches, 162, 164
Need(s), 16, 17, 24, 26, 40, 41, 42, 47, 50, 59, 61, 63, 68, 70, 72, 87, 110, 119, 123, 133, 134, 138, 158
New Testament, 25, 128, 141, 151, 192, 193, 194, 198, 199
Newton, Henry Fort, 206
Nichols, J. Randall, 205
Non-Christians, 58, 67, 75
Nonmembers, 29–30, 38, 56, 70, 75, 76, 80
Notes, use of, 57, 90, 104, 122

Obedience, 125, 131, 141, 142, 144, 198–202
Occasion, sense of, 19–20, 111–112
Old Testament, 25, 125, 130, 141, 191, 199
Opportunities, evangelistic, 37, 39, 42–43, 51, 160; at funerals, 61, 62, 67–68, 70; at ordination

services, 74, 75, 76, 78, 80; at weddings, 54, 55, 56, 59, 60
Order of worship, 22–25, 27, 30, 31, 33, 38, 39, 81; for funeral, 67, 68, 69; for ordination, 77, 78; and the sacraments, 47, 51
Ordination service, 74–79, 151
Organist, 23–24, 31, 35–36, 37, 47, 48, 67, 69
Orthodox churches: *see* Eastern Orthodox churches

Page references, 18
Parking, 40
Participants, 10, 18, 20, 38, 39, 79, 159–160; in funeral services, 64, 69; in ordination and installation services, 75, 76, 78, 79, 80–81; sacraments, 46, 47, 49, 51; in weddings, 55, 56, 59, 60; *see also* Congregation, participation of
Passion, 87–88
Pastor as Evangelist, The, 9, 10, 44, 203, 206
Pastor-evangelist, 9–10, and passim; as preacher, 83–160; as worship leader, 13–81
Pastoral ministry, 26, 28, 42–43, 79, 80; at time of death, 61–73; *see also* Minister; Ministry
Patience, 118, 141
Paul (apostle), 129, 136, 137–138, 160, 196, and chapter 10
Pentecost, 31, 198–202
Peter (apostle), 75, 199; and chapter 10
Pharisees, 153
Pittenger, Norman, 204
Plagiarism, 156–157
Planning, 26, 33–34, 38; advantages of, 93–95; of funerals, 64–65, 66, 72; of preaching, 92–108; of weddings, 57–58
Pluralism, 163–164, 169
Poetry, 99–100
Polity, 18, 46, 49, 78, 79, 159
Poor, the, 145, 168
Power, 62, 75, 107, 116, 135, 138, 143, 147, 149, 150, 152, 154, 155–156, 170, 197

Prayer: importance of, 89–91, 92, 97, 122, 135, 172, 201; at funerals, 64, 67, 68, 71; at ordinations, 77; at weddings, 55, 58

Prayers, corporate, 20, 24, 26, 33, 35, 37, 52, 125, 126

Preaching, 10, 26, 34, 39; attitude toward, 149–160; at baptism, 53; burden of, 157–160, 207; at communion, 49; context, 125–126, 204; direction, 118–121; evangelistic, 85–88, 109–122, 123, 125, 132, 141, 146, 147, 204; as event, 149–150; at funerals, 61, 62, 67–68; importance of, 150–152; manuscript, 103–104; method, 121–122; neglecting, 158–160; planning, 92–108, 189–191; preparation, 90, 103–104; at weddings, 57

Preparing the congregation: for baptism, 50–51; for communion, 47, 58; for decision, 118; for new hymns, 30, 31, 35, 36, 37; for innovation, 39–40; for weddings, 55; for worship, 95, 114, 118

Preparing the preacher: 77, 85–91, 92, 158; for preaching, 103–104

Presbyterian(s), 21, 24, 46, 49, 50–51, 77–78, 162–163, 170, 171, 198, 203, 207, 208

Presuppositions: *see* Assumptions

Proclamation, 77, 85, 116, 124, 131–132, 148, 149, 169

Proof(s), 128, 154, 171–172, 193

Protestants, 16, 45, 46, 58, 75, 164, 168

Pulpit: friendliness in, 18, 115, 116; in or out of, 57, 90, 107–108, 113, 159; interaction between pulpit and pew, 61, 86, 111–112, 121, 133; layperson in pulpit, 159; use of manuscript in, 101, 104, 106; views of, 15, 89, 115–116, 156, 172

Questions, 17–18, 32, 48–49, 61,

67, 77, 87, 110, 133, 134, 138, 159, 164, 169, 185, 186, 193

Reformed, 24, 45, 50, 170

Repentance, 85–86, 123, 141–142, 149

Response(s), 17, 18, 29, 37, 62, 77, 118, 121, 123, 127, 129, 175

Responsive reading, 18, 34

Resurrection, 61, 67, 128, 131, 136, 141, 183, 192–197

Revivalism, 110–111

Ritual, 15–16, 45, 47, 58, 75, 76, 77; of friendship, 41, 49

Robe: *see* Clerical garb

Roman Catholic, 16, 45, 75, 81, 162

Routley, Erik, 204

Sacrament(s), 24, 45–53, 58, 74, 75; *see also* Baptism; Holy Communion

Salvation, 53, 61, 67, 87, 139–143, 145

Sangster, W. E., 87, 204, 206

Schedule: sermon, 34, 92–95, 102, 190–191; worship, 34, 38, 51

Schindler, Alexander, 163

Schonfeld, Hugh, 194

Science, 129

Scribes, 152, 153

Scriptures: 18–19, 20, 33, 34, 155; authority of, 171, 192; in funerals, 64, 68, 70–71; ideas from, 95–96; planning, 94, 95; in preaching, 106–107; in weddings, 57; witness of, 128, 129–130

Seasons of church year, 25, 31, 38, 92, 96

Senn, Frank C., 18, 203

Sensitivity, evangelistic, 32, 34, 37, 38–39, 58, 66, 74, 79, 86–87, 88, 101, 109, 110, 111–112, 118, 121, 122, 123

Series, sermon, 92–93, 120

Sermon(s), 26, 86, 87, 88, 90, 91, 92, 95, 97, 98; communion, 47, 96; content of, 107–148; direction of, 119–121;

evangelistic, 86, 87, 108, 117, 123, 124, 125–126; expository, 106; first-person, 114–115, 191–196; hymns in, 35; installation, 80; manuscript, 101–106; ordination, 77; placement of, 24–25, 125–126; preparation, 60, 89–90, 92, 93, 101–106, 114; reproduction of, 102; teaching, 102; topical, 106–107, 111; in weddings, 57; as worship, 125, 204

Service Evangelism, 10, 206

Sin(s), 123, 131, 134–135, 136, 139, 140, 141, 145, 146, 147, 157

Sincerity, 18, 21, 75, 81, 90, 103, 131, 133, 147, 154, 157, 172

Singing, 30–34, 35, 36, 37, 48; at funerals, 65, 67, 69; at ordination service, 78

Sloyan, Gerard S., 204

Smiling, 18, 20, 47

Social action, 167–168; *see also* Gospel, social

Southern, Eileen, 204

Special services, 37–40

Stewart, James S., 25, 203–204

Stories, 100–101, 127, 129

Stowe, David, 164, 170–171, 206, 207

Stranger(s), 15, 16, 17, 19, 31, 40, 41, 46, 59, 110

Style: evangelistic, 162; of ordination bulletin, 78; preacher's, 11, 16, 23, 99, 112–118, 120; re weddings, 55, 57, 58; re worship, 39

Sweazey, George E., 85, 109, 204, 205, 206

Tannenbaum, Marc, 163

Teaching, 30, 32, 51, 55, 56, 102, 104, 155–156, 160, 161, 165–166, 170; *see also* Instruction; Interpretation; Training

Telephone: network, 65; number, 27, 28, 29, 174

Tennyson, Alfred, Lord, 186–187, 208

Terms, defining, 23

Theme: of Jesus' preaching, 123–124; of sermon, 47, 92–93, 94, 96, 98, 99, 107, 120, 125; *see also* Worship, theme of

Theology: of baptism, 50, 51; discourse, 89, 113; of evangelism, 10–11, 17, 81, 161–173; growth in, 94, 103; of hymns, 33; liberation, 145–146; narrative, 101, 127; of ordination, 75–77; personal, 70, 81, 116, 117, 155, 165–166; of the sacraments, 45–46

Title(s), sermon, 94, 97–98

Tizard, Leslie J., 205

Topic(s), sermon, 93, 94, 95, 102, 122

Tradition(s), 15, 17, 18, 39, 55, 75, 77, 152, 153, 169

Training: aides, 42; communion servers, 47; congregation, 40–41, 47–48; greeters, 41; ministers, 77, 155, 165–166, 169–170; ushers, 17, 41–42, 58–59, 65; worship participants, 17, 20–21

Trinity, 124, 198–202

Unchurched, 38, 56, 67, 70, 75, 80, 110–111, 141, 143, 164

Undertaker(s), 63, 68, 69–70

Urgency, 86, 90, 117–118, 123, 125, 158, 162

Ushers, 17, 20, 41–42, 58–59, 65, 175

Variety, 24, 34, 39–40, 46, 48, 93, 113–115

Vestments: *see* Clerical garb

Visitors, to church, 15–17, 19, 22, 23, 25, 28–29, 30, 31, 32, 40, 41, 42, 43, 46, 49, 53, 66, 75, 79, 80, 93, 95, 101, 120, 126; welcoming, 23, 28, 42, 46, 47, 126, 175

Vows: baptism, 50, 51; membership, 50, 133;

ordination, 75, 76, 77; wedding, 54, 57

Wagner, C. Peter, 167, 168, 207
Warmth, 17, 18, 57, 79, 115–116
Watkins, Keith, 203
Watts, Isaac, 31
Weatherspoon, Jesse Burton, 206
Webster, Douglas, 206
Weddings, 54–60
Welcome: see Visitors
White, James F., 203
Willimon, William H., 203
Winter, Gibson, 168, 207
Witnesses, 147–148, 162; to the gospel, 127–131
World, 9, 25, 71, 94, 119, 125, 136–137, 163
World Council of Churches, 162
Worship, 10, 15–81; balance in, 24–25, 30, 33, 34, 47; baptism, 50–53; before and after, 17, 40–43; clarity, 23, 25, 46, 77; communion, 25, 45–50, 58; as

context for evangelism, 54, 74, 77, 110–111, 125–126; innovative services, 37–40; movement of, 19, 22, 119–121; participants in, 20, 64, 75–76, 80–81, 95, 97; schedule, 34, 38, 51, 93, 105; sermon, 24–25, 26, 47, 77, 80, 92–95, 97–98; smoothness, 22–23; special services, 37–40; Sunday, 15, 22–44; theme of, 22, 25–26, 31, 33, 35, 36, 38, 53, 57, 78, 94; unity in, 19, 22, 26, 94, 125; weddings, 55, 56–59
Worship committee, 17–18, 48–50
Worship leader, 9, 10, 15, 16–21, 81, 111, 126; Sunday, 22–26, 33, 34, 35, 36, 37, 45; funerals, 63, 69; weddings, 54, 56

Year, Christian: see Seasons of church year
Young, Robert D., 205, 206

Zip Code, 29, 174